G000292524

AUSTRIA & SWITZERLAND

contents

Map pages	ii
Map symbols	iii
Route planner	iv
Distance chart	I
Road atlas	**2-39**
Index and city environs plans	**40-60**

Bern	41	Salzburg	56
Genève	46	Wien	59
Milano	50	Zürich	60
Roma	54		

1st edition February 1996

© The Automobile Association 1996

Published by AA Publishing (a trading name of Automobile Association Developments Limited, whose registered office is Norfolk House, Priestley Road, Basingstoke, Hampshire, RG24 9NY. Registered number 1878835).

Mapping produced by the Cartographic Department of The Automobile Association. This atlas has been compiled and produced from the Automaps database utilising electronic and computer technology.

ISBN 0 7495 1188 5

A CIP catalogue for this book is available from the British Library.

Printed in Great Britain by BPC Waterlow Ltd, Dunstable.

The contents of this atlas are believed correct at the time of printing. Nevertheless, the publishers cannot accept any responsibility for errors or omissions or for changes in the details given. They would welcome information to help keep this atlas up to date, please write to the Cartographic Editor, Publishing Division, The Automobile Association, Norfolk House, Priestley Road, Basingstoke, Hampshire, RG24 9NY.

map pages

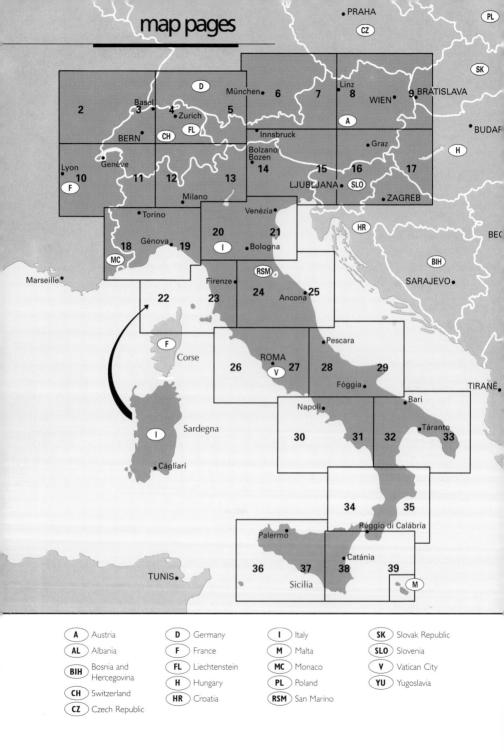

A	Austria	**D**	Germany	**I**	Italy	**SK**	Slovak Republic
AL	Albania	**F**	France	**M**	Malta	**SLO**	Slovenia
BIH	Bosnia and Hercegovina	**FL**	Liechtenstein	**MC**	Monaco	**V**	Vatican City
CH	Switzerland	**H**	Hungary	**PL**	Poland	**YU**	Yugoslavia
CZ	Czech Republic	**HR**	Croatia	**RSM**	San Marino		

map symbols

Toll motorways

(A55) (E55)	Dual carriageway with road numbers
	Single carriageway
	Interchange
	Restricted interchange
(S)	Service area
	Under construction

Non-toll motorways

(A55) (E55)	Dual carriageway with road numbers
	Single carriageway
	Interchange
	Restricted interchange
(S)	Service area
	Under construction

National roads

SS45	Dual carriageway with road number
	Single carriageway

Regional roads

SS45	Dual carriageway with road number
	Single carriageway

Local roads

SS453	Dual carriageway with road number
	Single carriageway
D28	Minor road with road number
38	Page overlap and number

Symbols

(E55) E55	European international network numbers
	Motorway in tunnel
	Road in tunnel
	Road under construction
	Toll point
24	Distances in kilometres
>>	Gradient 14% and over
>	Gradient 6%-13%
10-6 Furkapass 2431	Mountain pass with closure period
628 PUERTO DE ANGER	Spot height (metres)
	Ferry route (all year)
	Hovercraft (all year)
	Airport (International)
	Car transporter (rail)
	Mountain railway
	Viewpoint (180° or 360°)
	Urban area
	Town location
	Canal
	Wooded area

Boundaries

	International
	National
	Unrecognised international
	Restricted frontier crossing

scale

1:1 000 000   10 kilometres : 1 centimetre

0	10	20	30	40	50 kilometres
0		10		20	30 miles

16 miles : 1 inch

route planner

Catánia - Táranto = 472km

472

Cities (diagonal labels, in order):

Ancona (I), Bari (I), Basel (CH), Bern (CH), Bologna (I), Bolzano/Bozen (I), Bréscia (I), Brindisi (I), Cágliari (I), Catánia (I), Firenze (I), Fóggia (I), Genève (CH), Génova (I), Graz (A), Innsbruck (A), Klagenfurt (A), Linz (A), Ljubljana (SLO), Messina (I), Milano (I), München (D), Napoli (I), Nice (F), Palermo (I), Perúgia (I), Pescara (I), Pisa (I), Réggio di Calábria (I), Roma (I), Salzburg (A), Sassari (I), Strasbourg (F), Táranto (I), Torino (I), Venézia (I), Verona (I), Wien (A), Zagreb (HR), Zürich (CH)

Distance matrix (lower triangle — each row lists distances from that city to the preceding cities, in the order listed above):

From \ To	Ancona	Bari	Basel	Bern	Bologna	Bolzano	Bréscia	Brindisi
Bari	468							
Basel	767	1221						
Bern	784	1238	92					
Bologna	217	671	549	566				
Bolzano	496	950	503	520	278			
Bréscia	392	846	420	437	174	195		
Brindisi	579	112	1332	1349	782	1061	957	
Cágliari	422	263	1061	652	479	735	575	374

*

1

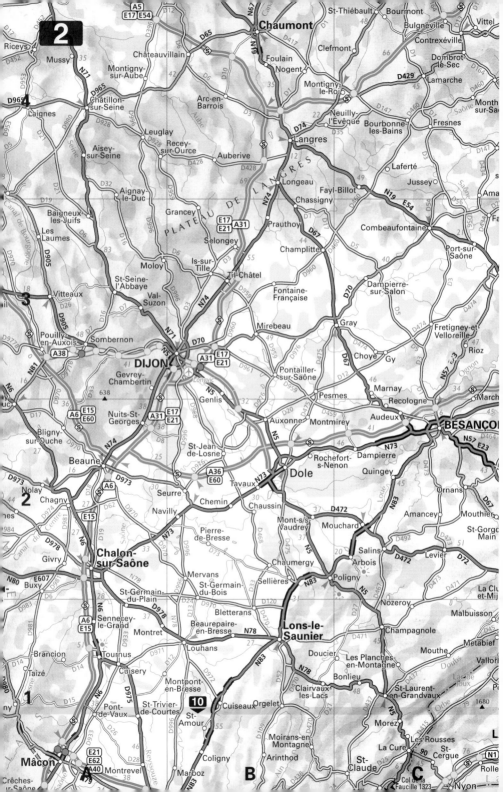

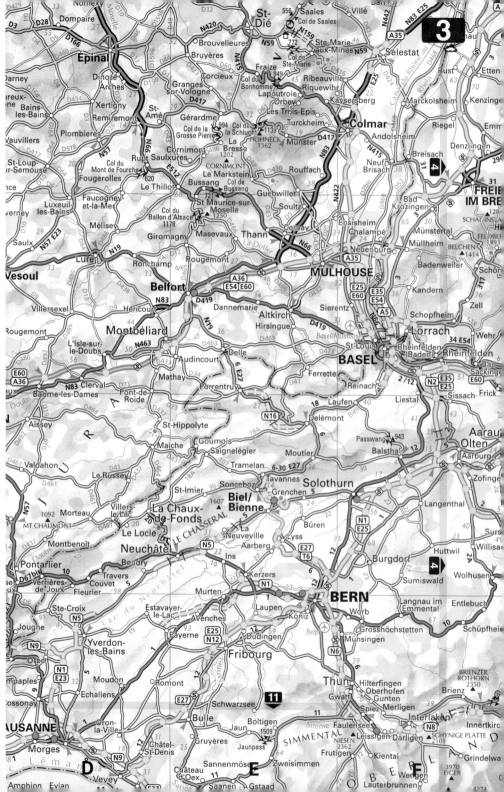

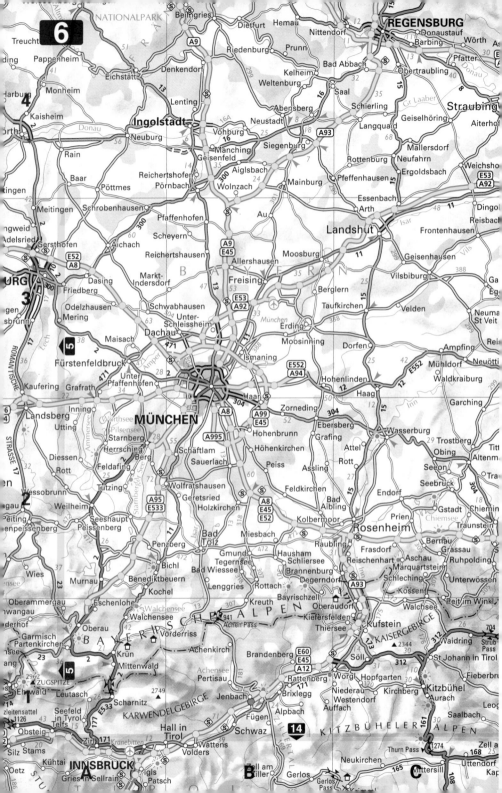

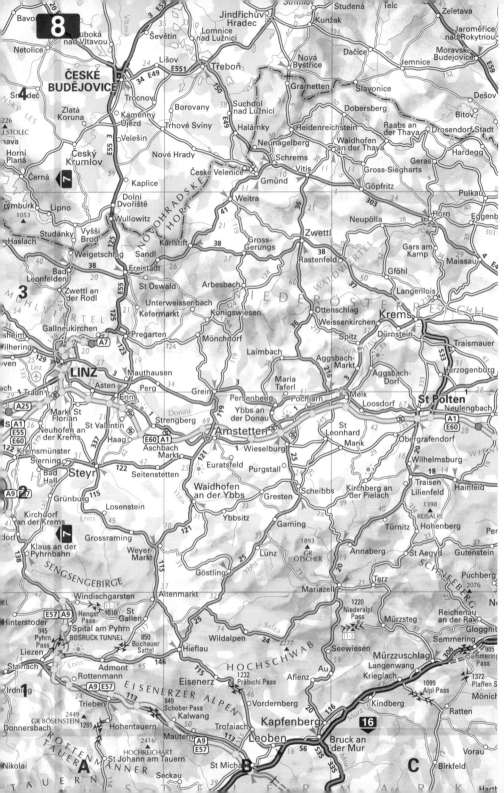

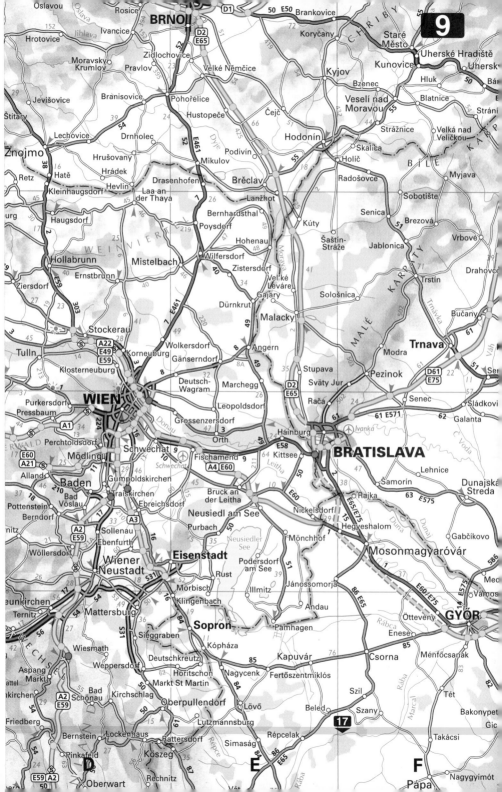

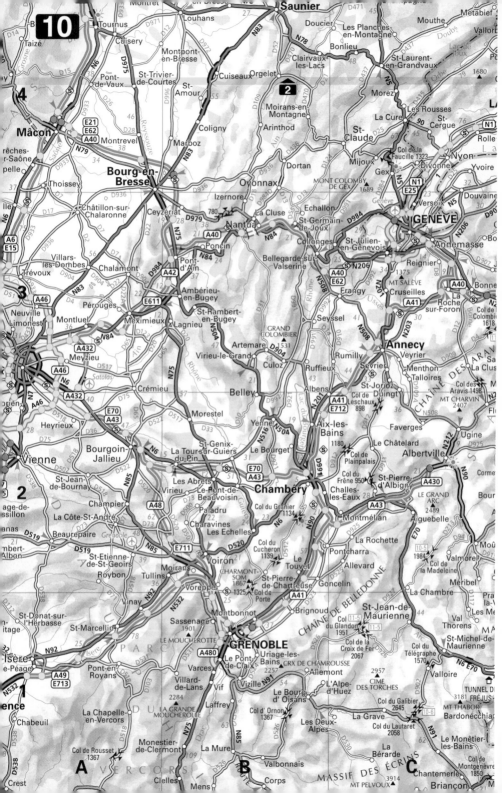

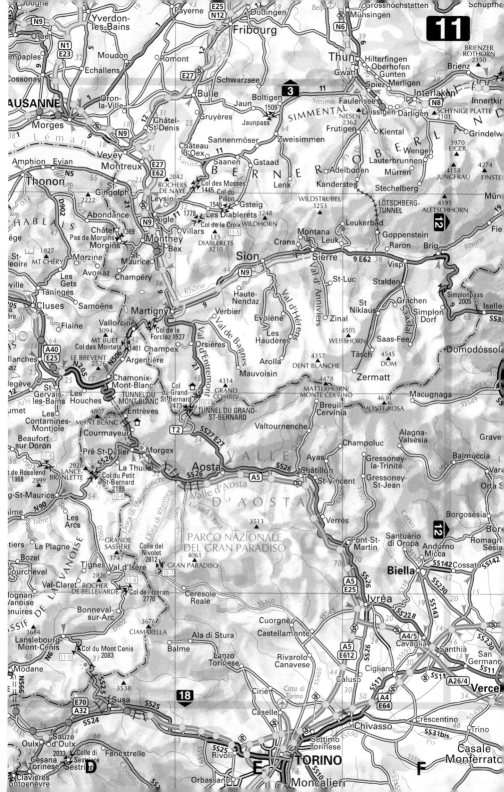

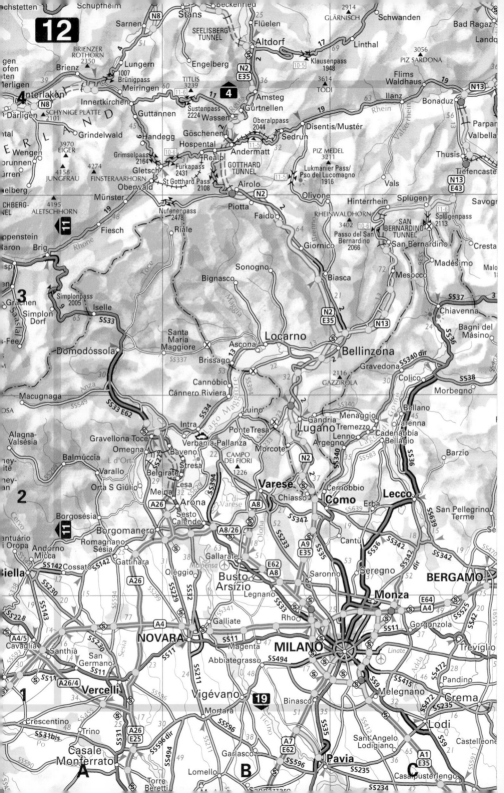

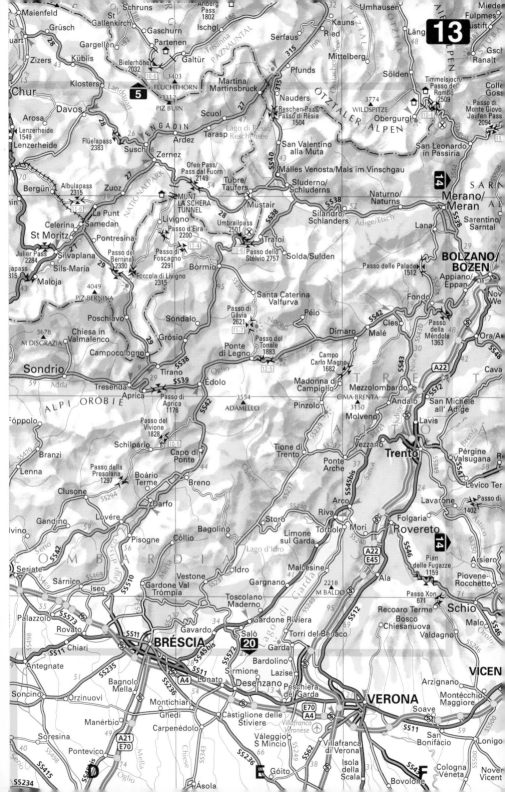

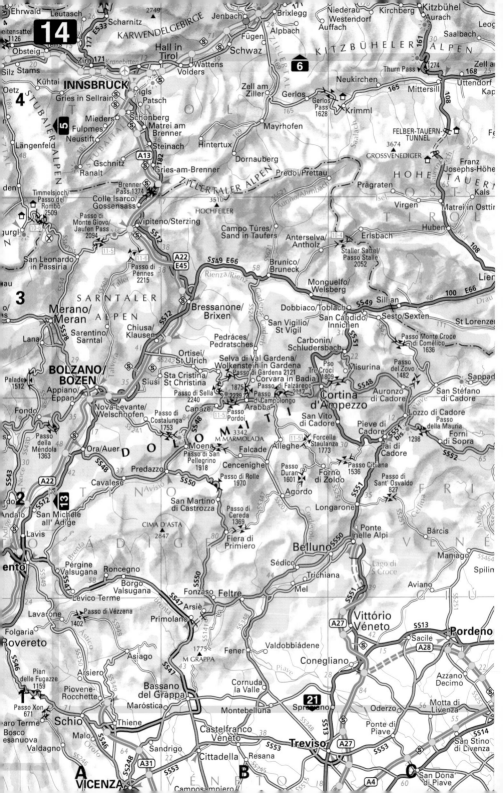

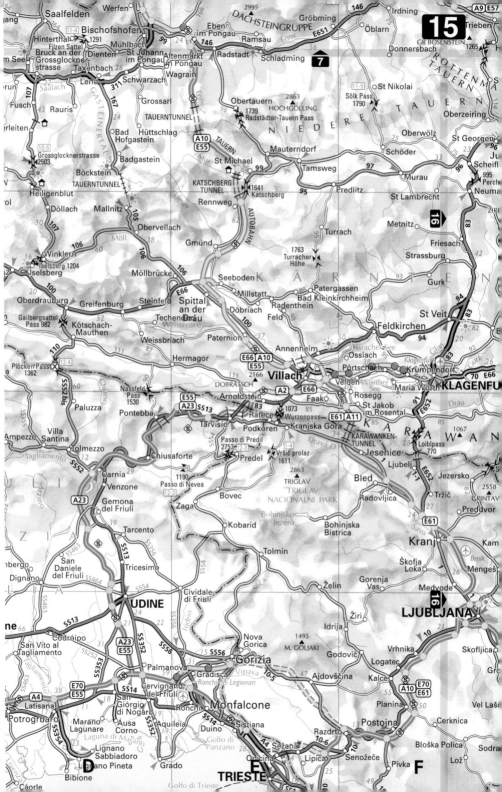

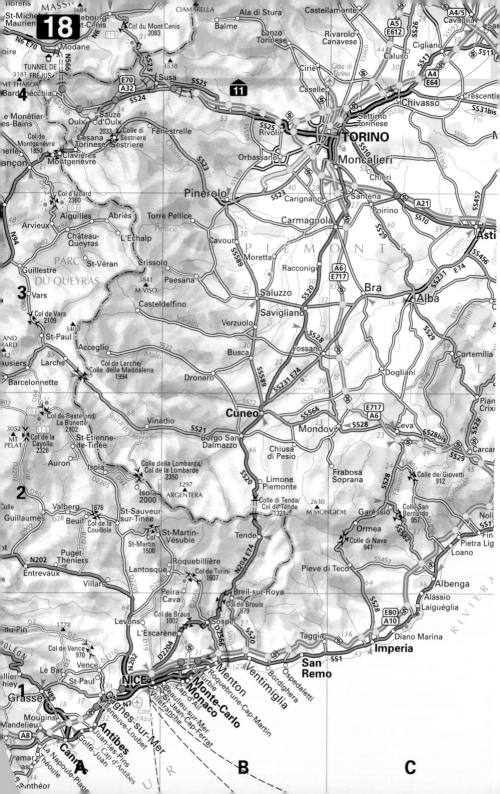

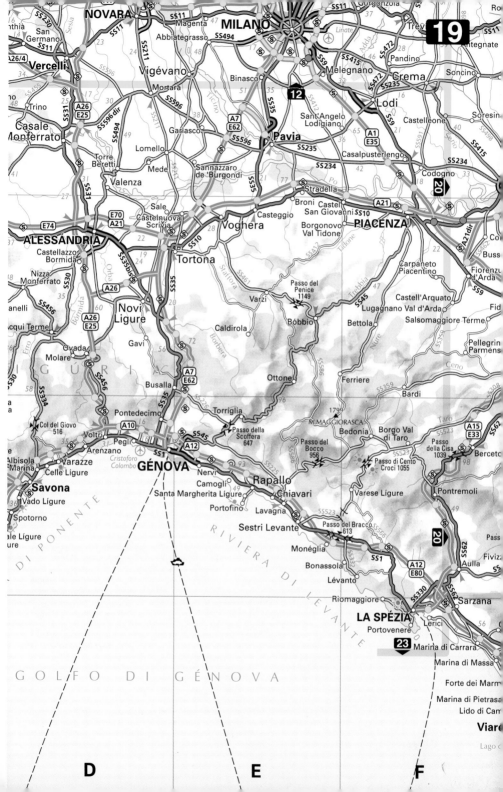

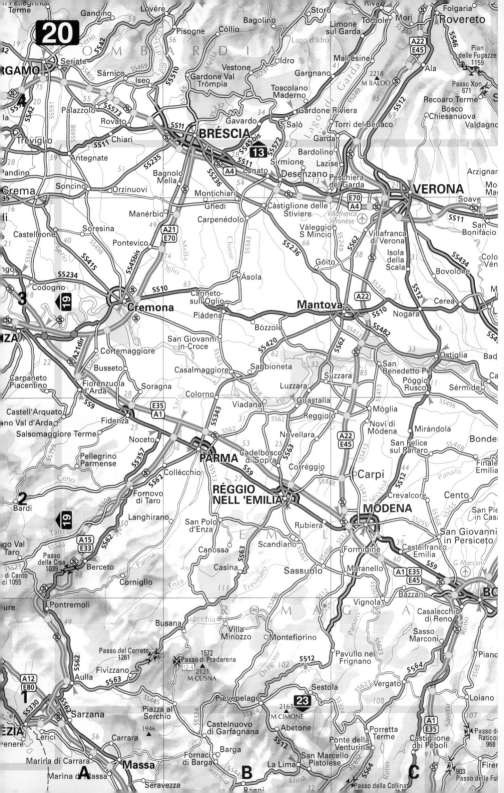

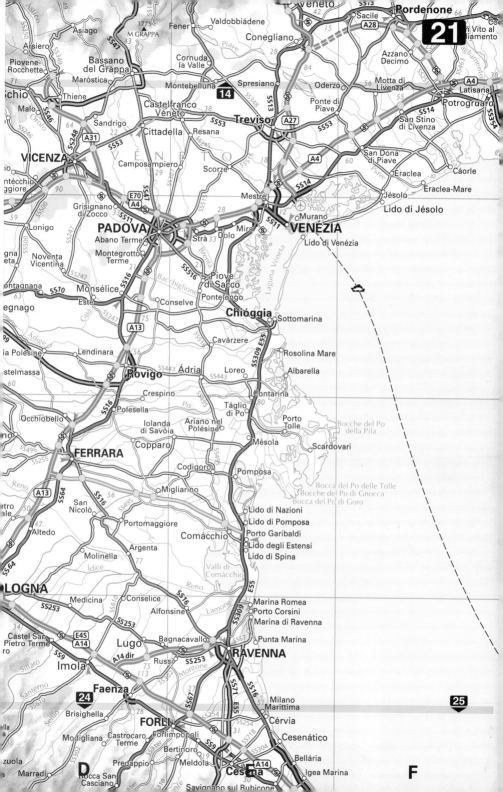

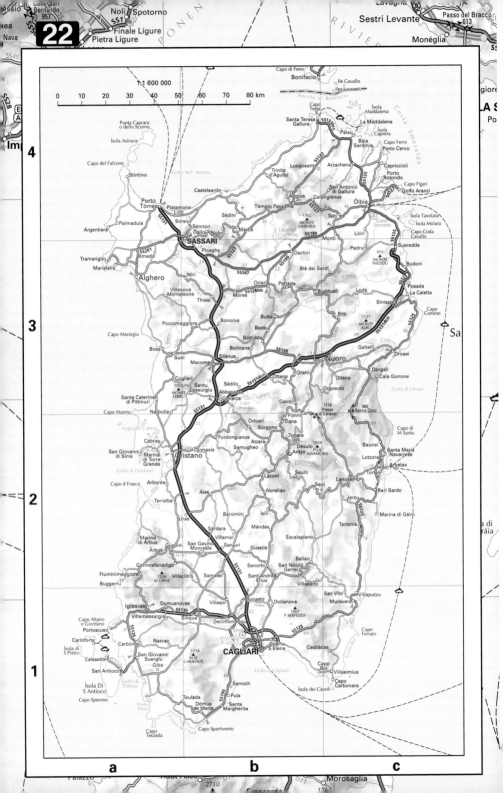

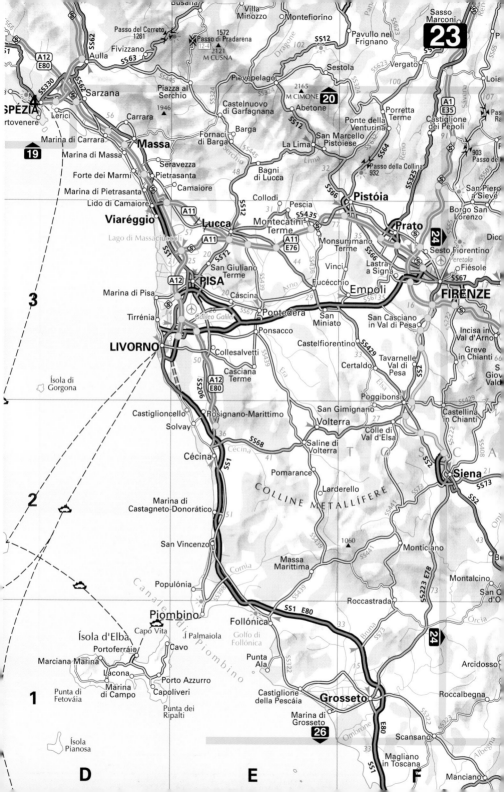

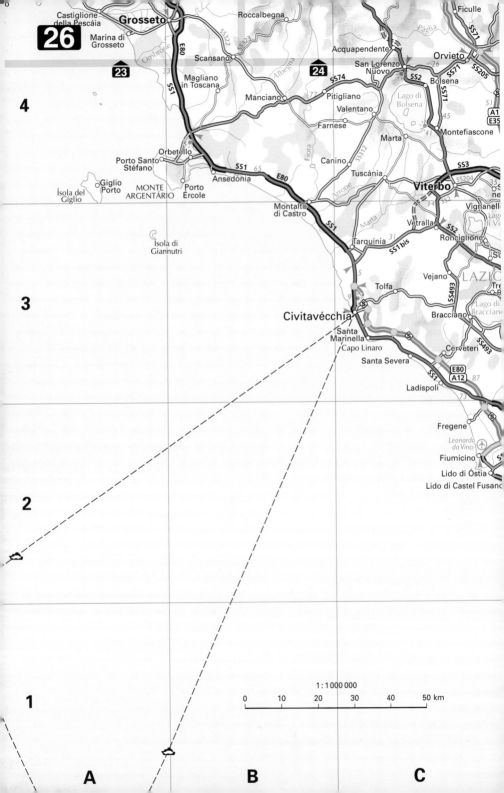

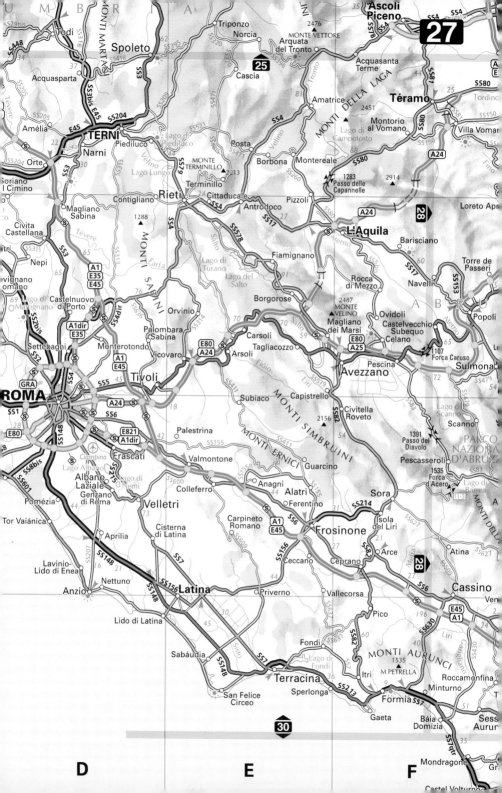

Vela Luka

Kor

Sušac

Las

Í Pianosa

Í Capráia

ÍSOLE TRÉMITI

Í S Dómino

arino

Marina di Chiéuti

Lido di
Torre Mileto

Rodi
Gargánico

Peschici

14
55

S

Lago di Lesina

SS89 35

Lesina

Lago di
Varano

Vico del
Gargano

40

Vieste

Fortore

22

SS89

Sannicandro
Garganico

Cagnano
Varano

SS28

SS89

SS16ter

54

Apricena

PROMONTORIO DEL GARGANO

SS272

1055

Monte
Sant'angelo

Mattinata

79

San Marco
in Lamis

San Giovanni
Rotondo

55

SS89

remaggiore

**San
Severo**

S

Manfredónia

astelnuovo
lla Dáunia

SS160

29

39

Golfo di
Manfredónia

Candelaro

Lucera

SS16

SS589

SS159

48

SS17

Cervaro

44

SS545

Zapponeta

FOGGIA

S

SS544

SS159

Margherita
di Savoia

meo

Celone

23

Orta
Nova

50

SS16

Trinitapoli

SS16

Barletta

Troia

SS160

Castellúccio
dei Sáuri

SS545

San Ferdinando
di Puglia

34

Giardinetto

48

56

SS161

13

SS545

SS16

Trani

Biscéglie

SS90

SS655

Carapelle

Cerignola

Canosa di Puglia

SS93

Andria

A14
E55

32

Molfetta

Savignano
Irpino

31

Ascoli
Satriano

SS98

Corato

S

Ruvo di
Puglia

12

Giovinazzo

SS16

SS91B

Candela

A16
E842

Lago di
Capacciotti

SS93

Ofanto

SS97

SS98

Bitonto

72

D

E

Minervino

F

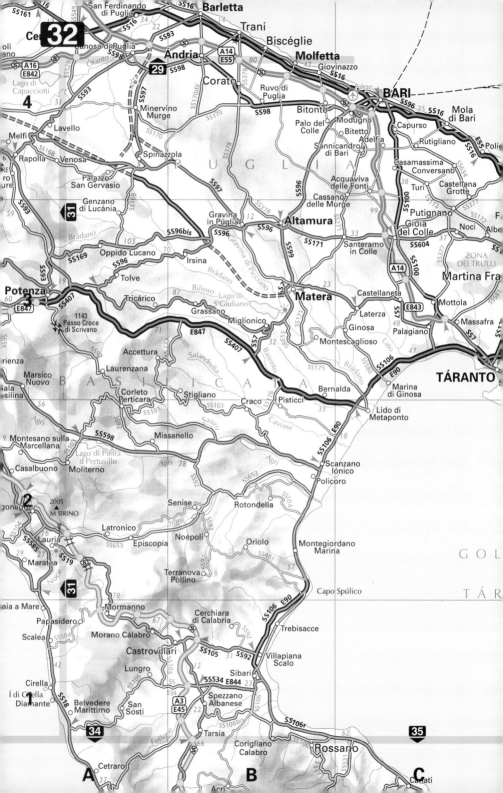

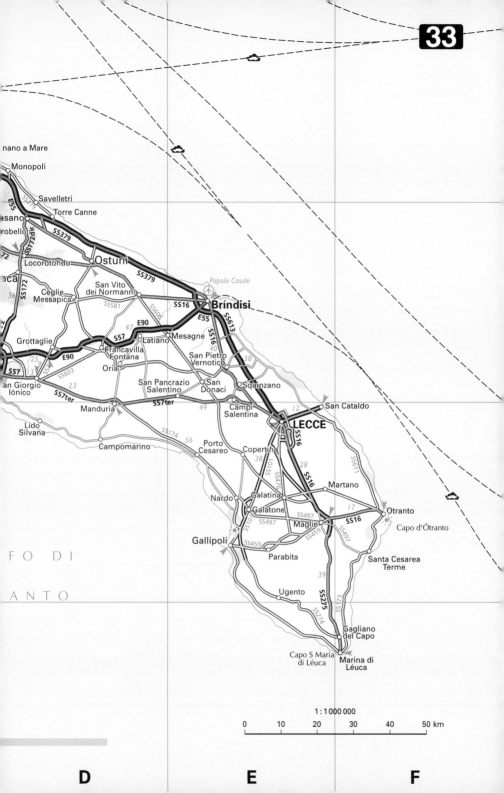

4

31

1 : 1 000 000

| 0 | 10 | 20 | 30 | 40 | 50 km |

3

Í Strómboli

ÍSOLE EÓLIE O LÍPARI

Í Panarea

icudi

Í Salina

2

Í Lípari

Í Vulcano

Í di Cirella
Diamante
Cirellà
SS18
Belvedere
Marittimo

Cetr

Paola

San Lucid

Amar

Campora San Giov

Tropea
Vibo Val
Capo Vaticano
Mile

42

Rosarno
Gióia Táuro
SS18
Palmi
Taurianova
Opp
Man

Bagnara
Calabria
A3
E45

Sparta SS114dit 102
Torre
Faro
Scilla SS18
Sinopoli
Villa San Giovanni
Delianuova
ASPROMONT
Gámbárie
1955
MONTALTO

Villafianca
Tirrena

C di Milazzo
Milazzo
SS113 102
A20
MESSINA
Santa
Lucia del Mela
Tremestieri
RÉGGIO DI
CALABRIA

Gioiosa C Calava
Marea
Castroreale
Terme
Galati
Marina

Capo
d'Orlando
Brolo
Castroreale
A18
E45
SS114

Sant'Ágata
Militello
A20
E90
Naso
SS116
Falcone
Novara
di Sicilia
Ali Terme
SS106 E90
SS83

San
Fratello
SS289
Tortorici
Ucria
1287
PZO DI VERNA
Roccalumera
Santa Teresa
di Riva

É B R O D I
1264
Portella
Mandrazzi
1125
MONTI PELORITANI
31
Bova
Marina

1847
M SORO
Portella dello
Zoppo
48

Lago
emmina Morta
1524
d'Ancipa
Randazzo
Francavilla
di Sicilia
Alcantara
Melito di
Porto Salv

Cesarò
A
B
Taormina
Mazzaró
C

38
SS113

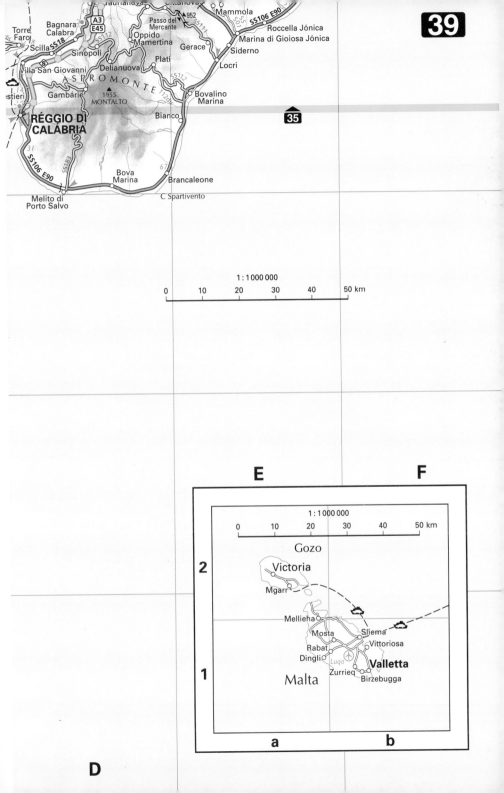

Torre Faro

Bagnara Calabria

Scilla

Sinopoli

Villa San Giovanni

Delianuova

Oppido Mamertina

Gerace

Plati

Gambárie

A S P R O M O N T E

1955 MONTALTO

RÉGGIO DI CALÁBRIA

Bianco

Bova Marina

Melito di Porto Salvo

Brancaleone

C Spartivento

Mammola

Passo del Mercante

Roccella Jónica

Marina di Gioiosa Jónica

Siderno

Locri

Bovalino Marina

35

SS518

SS106 E90

SS112

A3

E45

952

SS106 E90

SS183

SS106 E90

31

67

1:1 000 000

0   10   20   30   40   50 km

E

F

1:1 000 000

0   10   20   30   40   50 km

Gozo

Victoria

Mgarr

Mellieha

Mosta

Rabat

Dingli

Zurrieq

Luqa

Sliema

Vittoriosa

Valletta

Birzebugga

Malta

2

1

a

b

D

A

Aarau CH 4 A2
Aarberg CH 3 E2
Aarburg CH 4 A2
Abano Terme I 21 D3
Abbasanta I 22 b3
Abbiategrasso I .... 12 BI
Abensberg D 6 B4
Abetone I 23 E4
Abondance F .... II D3
Abriès F 18 A3
Abtenau A .... 7 EI
Acate I 38 A2
Acceglio I 18 A3
Accettura I 32 A3
Acciaroli I 31 E2
Acerno I 31 E3
Achenkirch A .... 6 BI
Aci Castello I 38 C3
Aci Trezza I 38 C3
Acireale I 38 C3
Acqualagna I 24 C3
Acquapendente I .... 24 BI
Acquasanta Terme I .... 25 EI
Acquasparta I 27 D4
Acquaviva delle Fonti I 32 C4
Acqui Terme I 19 D3
Acri I 35 D4
Adelboden CH .... II E4
Adelfia I 32 C4
Adelsried D 5 F4
Admont A .... 8 AI
Adrano I 38 B3
Ádria I 21 E3
Aflenz A .... 8 BI
Agay F .... 18 AI
Aggius I 22 b4
Aggsbach-Dorf A 8 C3
Aggsbach-Markt A 8 C3
Agira I 38 A3
Agnone I 28 B2
Agordo I 14 B2
Agrigento I 37 D2
Agropoli I 31 E2
Aicha D 7 E3
Aichach D 6 A3
Aidenbach D 7 D3
Aidone I 37 F3
Aigen A 7 F3
Aigle CH .... II D3
Aiglsbach D 6 B4
Aignay-le-Duc F 2 A4
Aiguebelle F 10 C2
Aiguilles F 18 A3
Aime F .... II D2
Airolo CH 12 B4
Aisey-sur-Seine F 2 A4
Aissey F 3 D2
Aiterhofen D 7 D4
Aitrach D 5 E3
Aix-les-Bains F 10 B2
Ajdovščina SLO .... 15 EI
Ajka H 17 F4
Ala I 13 F2
Alà dei Sardi I 22 c3
Ala di Stura I .... II EI
Alagna-Valsésia I .... II F2
Alássio I .... 18 CI
Alatri I 27 E2
Alba I 18 C3
Alba Adriatica I .... 25 EI
Albano Laziale I 27 D2
Albarella I 21 E3
Albenga I 18 C2
Albens F 10 B2
Alberobello I 32 C3
Albertville F 10 C2
Albisola Marina I 19 D2
Álcamo I 36 C4

Áles I 22 b2
Alessándria I 19 D3
Alessándria della Rocca I 37 D3
Alfedena I 28 A2
Alfonsine I .... 21 EI
Alghero I 22 a3
Ali Terme I 38 C4
Ália I 37 D3
Alimena I 37 E3
Alkoven A 7 F3
Alland A 9 D2
Álleghe I 14 B2
Allemont F .... 10 BI
Allensbach D 4 C3
Allershausen D 6 B3
Allevard F 10 C2
Alpbach A .... 6 BI
Alpirsbach D 4 B4
Altamura I 32 B3
Altaussee A .... 7 EI
Altdorf CH .... 4 BI
Altedo I 21 D2
Altenmarkt A .... 8 AI
Altenmarkt D 6 C2
Altenmarkt im Pongau A .... 7 EI
Altenstadt D 5 E4
Altheim A 7 D3
Altkirch F 3 E3
Altmünster A 7 E2
Altötting D 7 D3
Altshausen D 5 D3
Altstätten CH 5 D2
Amalfi I 31 D3
Amance F 2 C4
Amancey F 2 C2
Amandola I .... 25 DI
Amantea I 35 D3
Amatrice I 27 E4
Ambérieu-en-Bugey F 10 B3
Amélia I 27 D4
Ampezzo I 15 D2
Ampfing D 6 C3
Amphion F .... II D4
Amriswil CH 4 C2
Amsteg CH 12 B4
Amstetten A 8 B2
Anagni I 27 E2
Ancona I 25 E3
Andalo I 13 F2
Andau A .... 9 EI
Andermatt CH 12 B4
Andolsheim F 3 F4
Andorno Micca I .... II F2
Andretta I 31 E4
Ándria I .... 29 FI
Anger A 16 C4
Angern A 9 E3
Annaberg A .... 7 EI
Annaberg A 8 C2
Annecy F 10 C3
Annemasse F 10 C3
Annenheim A 15 E3
Ansedónia I 26 B4
Antegnate I 20 A4
Anterselva/Antholz I 14 B3
Anthéor F .... 18 AI
Antholz/Anterselva I 14 B3
Antibes F .... 18 AI
Antrodoco I 27 E3
Anzio I 27 D2
Aosta I .... II E2
Apécchio I 24 C3
Appenzell CH 4 C2
Appiano/Eppan I 14 A2
Aprica I 13 D3
Apricena I 29 D2
Aprilia I 27 D2
Aquileia I .... 15 DI
Arabba I 14 B2
Aragona I 37 D3
Arbatax I 22 c2
Arbesbach A 8 B3
Arbois F 2 C2

Arbon CH 4 C2
Arboréa I 22 a2
Árbus I 22 a2
Arc-en-Barrois F 2 B4
Arce I 27 F2
Arcévia I 25 D2
Arches F 3 D4
Arcidosso I .... 24 AI
Arco I 13 F2
Ardez CH 13 E4
Arenzano I 19 D2
Arezzo I 24 B2
Argegno I 12 C2
Argenta I 21 D2
Argentiera I 22 a4
Argentière F .... II D3
Ariano Irpino I 31 E4
Ariano nel Polésine I 21 E2
Arinthod F 10 B4
Aritzo I 22 b2
Arnay-le-Duc F 2 A2
Arnoldstein A 15 E2
Arolla CH .... II E3
Arona I 12 B2
Arosa CH 13 D4
Arquata del Tronto I .... 25 DI
Arsiè I .... 14 BI
Arsiero I .... 14 AI
Arsoli I 27 E3
Artemare F 10 B3
Arth CH 4 B2
Arth D 6 C3
Arvieux F 18 A3
Arzachena I 22 c4
Arzignano I 21 D4
Arzl A 5 F2
Ascha D 7 D4
Aschach A 7 F3
Aschau D 6 C2
Aschbach Markt A 8 B2
Asco F .... 22 BI
Áscoli Piceno I .... 25 EI
Ascoli Satriano I .... 29 DI
Ascona CH 12 B3
Asiago I .... 14 AI
Asola I 20 B3
Aspang Markt A .... 9 DI
Assisi I .... 24 CI
Assling D 6 B2
Asten A 8 A3
Asti I 18 C3
Atina I 28 A2
Attel D 6 C2
Attersee A 7 E2
Attnang-Puchheim A 7 E2
Atzara I 22 b2
Au A .... 8 CI
Au D 6 B3
Auberive F 2 B4
Audeux F 2 C2
Audincourt F 3 E3
Auer/Ora I 14 A2
Auffach A .... 6 BI
Augsburg D 5 F4
Augusta I 38 C2
Auletta I 31 E3
Aulla I .... 20 AI
Aurach A .... 6 CI
Auron F 18 A2
Auronzo di Cadore I 14 C3
Áusa Corno I .... 15 DI
Aussernbrünst D 7 E4
Auxonne F 2 B2
Avellino I 31 D4
Avenches CH .... 3 EI
Aversa I 30 C4
Avezzano I 27 F3
Aviano I 14 C2
Avola I .... 38 BI
Avoriaz F .... II D3
Ayas I .... II E2
Azzano Decimo I .... 14 CI

B

Baad A	5	E2
Baar D	6	A4
Babenhausen D	5	E4
Bacoli I	30	C3
Bad Abbach D	6	C4
Bad Aibling D	6	B2
Bad Aussee A	7	E1
Bad Buchau D	5	D3
Bad Dürrheim D	4	B4
Bad Gleichenberg A	16	C3
Bad Goisern A	7	E1
Bad Hall A	7	F2
Bad Hofgastein A	15	D4
Bad Ischl A	7	E1
Bad Kleinkirchheim A	15	E3
Bad Krozingen D	3	F3
Bad Leonfelden A	8	A3
Bad Mitterndorf A	7	F1
Bad Peterstal D	4	B4
Bad Ragaz CH	4	C1
Bad Reichenhall D	7	D2
Bad Rippoldsau D	4	B4
Bad Säckingen D	4	A3
Bad St. Leonhard A	16	B3
Bad Schallerbach A	7	F2

Bad Schönau A	9	D1
Bad Schussenried D	5	D3
Bad Tölz D	6	B2
Bad Urach D	5	D4
Bad Vöslau A	9	D2
Bad Waldsee D	5	D3
Bad Wiessee D	6	B2
Bad Wörishofen D	5	E3
Bad Wurzach D	5	D3
Badacsonytomaj H	17	F3
Baden A	9	D2
Baden CH	4	B2
Badenweiler D	3	F3
Badgastein A	15	D4
Badia Polésine I	21	D3
Badia Tedalda I	24	B3
Badolato Marina I	35	E2
Bagheria I	37	D4
Bagnacavallo I	21	D1
Bagnara Calabra I	34	C1
Bagni del Másino I	12	C3
Bagni di Lucca I	23	E4
Bagno di Romagna I	24	B3
Bagnolo Mella I	20	B4
Bagod H	17	E3
Bagolino I	13	E2
Báia Domizia I	28	A1
Báia Sardínia I	22	c4
Baiano I	31	D4
Baigneux-les-Juifs F	2	A3

Bains-les-Bains F	3	D4
Bajánsenye H	17	D3
Bak H	17	E3
Bakonygyepes H	17	F4
Balatonboglár H	17	F3
Balatonederics H	17	F3
Balatonkeresztúr H	17	F3
Balatonlelle H	17	F3
Balderschwang D	5	E2
Balingen D	4	C4
Ballao I	22	b2
Balme I	11	D1
Balmúccia I	12	A2
Balsthal CH	3	F2
Bánov CZ	9	F4
Barbing D	6	C4
Barcellona-Pozzo di Gotto I	34	B1
Barcelonnette F	18	A3
Bárcis I	14	C2
Barcs H	17	F1
Bardi I	19	F3
Bardolino I	20	C4
Bardonécchia I	18	A4
Barga I	23	E4
Bari I	32	C4
Bari Sardo I	22	c2
Barisciano I	27	F3
Barletta I	29	F1
Barr F	3	F4
Barrafranca I	37	E2

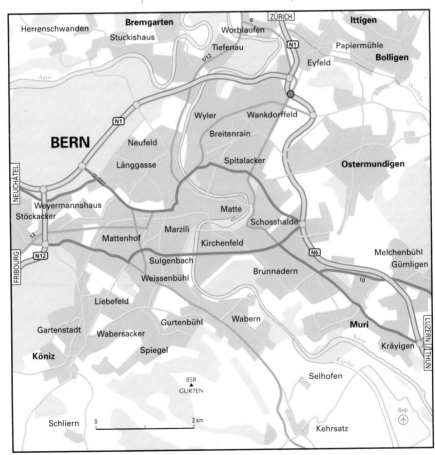

Barrea I	28	A2
Barúmini I	22	b2
Barzio I	12	C2
Basel CH	3	F3
Bassano del Grappa I	14	B1
Bastia I	22	C1
Battipáglia I	31	E3
Baume-les-Dames F	3	D3
Baunei I	22	c2
Baveno I	12	B2
Bavorov CZ	7	F4
Bayerisch Eisenstein D	7	E4
Bayrischzell D	6	B2
Bazzano I	20	C2
Beaufort sur Doron F	11	D2
Beaulieu-sur-Mer F	18	B1
Beaune F	2	A2
Beaurepaire F	10	A2
Beaurepaire-en-Bresse F	2	B1
Beckenried CH	4	B1
Becsehely H	17	E2
Bedonia I	19	F2
Beilngries D	6	B4
Beled H	9	E1
Belfort F	3	E3
Belgirate I	12	B2
Belgodère F	22	B1
Bellágio I	12	C2
Bellano I	12	C2
Bellária I	24	C4
Bellegarde-sur-Valserine F	10	B3
Belleville F	10	A3
Belley F	10	B2
Bellinzona CH	12	C3
Belluno I	14	C2
Belpasso I	38	B3
Beltinci SLO	17	D2
Belvedere Marittimo I	32	A1
Benediktbeuern D	6	A2
Benevento I	31	D4
Benfeld F	3	F4
Berceto I	20	A2
Berchtesgaden D	7	D1
Berek HR	17	E1
Berg D	6	A2
Bergamo I	12	C2
Berglern D	6	B3
Bergün CH	13	D4
Berkheim D	5	E3
Berlingen CH	4	C3
Bern CH	3	E1
Bernalda I	32	B3
Bernau D	6	C2
Berndorf A	9	D2
Bernhardsthal A	9	E3
Bernstein A	17	D4
Beromünster CH	4	A2
Bertinoro I	24	B4
Berwang A	5	F2
Besançon F	2	C2
Bettola I	19	F3
Beuil F	18	A2
Beuron D	4	C4
Bevagna I	24	C1
Bex CH	11	D3
Bezau A	5	D2
Bianco I	39	E4
Biasca CH	12	B3
Bibbiena I	24	B3
Biberach D	4	A4
Biberach an der Riss D	5	D3
Bibione I	15	D1
Bichl D	6	A2
Biel/Bienne CH	3	E2
Biella I	11	F2
Bienne/Biel CH	3	E2
Bignasco CH	12	B3
Binasco I	12	B1
Birkfeld A	16	C4
Birnau D	4	C3
Birzebugga M	39	b1
Biscéglie I	29	F1
Bischofshofen A	7	D1

Bitetto I	32	C4
Bitonto I	32	B4
Bitov CZ	8	C4
Bitti I	22	c3
Bivona I	37	D3
Bjelovar HR	17	E1
Blatnice CZ	9	F4
Blaubeuren D	5	D4
Blaustein D	5	D4
Bled SLO	15	F2
Bleiburg A	16	B3
Bletterans F	2	B1
Bligny-sur-Ouche F	2	A2
Bloška Polica SLO	16	A1
Bludenz A	5	D2
Blumberg D	4	B3
Boário Terme I	13	D2
Bobbio I	19	E3
Bobingen D	5	F4
Böckstein A	15	D4
Bodenmais D	7	D4
Bodman D	4	C3
Boëge F	10	C3
Bogen D	7	D4
Bohinjska Bistrica SLO	15	E2
Böhönye H	17	F2
Boiano I	28	B1
Bologna I	20	C1
Bolótana I	22	b3
Bolsena I	26	C4
Boltigen CH	11	E4
Bolzano/Bozen I	14	A3
Bonaduz CH	12	C4
Bonassola I	19	F2
Bondeno I	21	D2
Bonefro I	28	C2
Bonlieu F	2	C1
Bonndorf D	4	B3
Bonneval-sur-Arc F	11	D1
Bonneville F	10	C3
Bono I	22	b3
Bonorva I	22	b3
Borba I	27	E4
Bordighera I	18	B1
Borgo San Dalmazzo I	18	B2
Borgo San Lorenzo I	24	A3
Borgo Val di Taro I	19	F2
Borgo Valsugana I	14	A2
Borgomanero I	12	A2
Borgonovo Val Tidone I	19	F3
Borgorose I	27	E3
Borgosésia I	12	A2
Bórmio I	13	E3
Borovany CZ	8	B4
Bosa I	22	a3
Bosco Chiesanuova I	13	F1
Bottidda I	22	b3
Boudry CH	3	D2
Bourbonne-les-Bains F	2	C4
Bourg-de-Péage F	10	A1
Bourg-en-Bresse F	10	A4
Bourg-St-Maurice F	11	D2
Bourgoin-Jallieu F	10	A2
Bourmont F	2	C4
Bova Marina I	39	D4
Bovalino Marina I	35	D1
Bovec SLO	15	E2
Bovolone I	20	C3
Bozel F	11	D2
Bozen/Bolzano I	14	A3
Bózzolo I	20	B3
Bra I	18	C3
Bracciano I	26	C3
Brancaleone I	39	D4
Brancion F	2	A1
Brand A	5	D1
Brandenberg A	6	B1
Branišovice CZ	9	D4
Brankovice CZ	9	E4
Brannenburg D	6	C2
Branzi I	13	D2
Bratislava SK	9	E2
Braunau A	7	D3

Břeclav CZ	9	E4
Bregenz A	5	D2
Breil-sur-Roya F	18	B1
Breisach D	3	F4
Breno I	13	E2
Bréscia I	13	D1
Bressanone/Brixen I	14	B3
Breuil-Cervínia I	11	E2
Brežice SLO	16	C1
Breznica HR	17	D1
Brezová SK	9	F3
Briançon F	18	A4
Brienz CH	4	A1
Brienza I	31	F3
Brig CH	11	F3
Brignoud F	10	B1
Bríndisi I	33	E3
Brisighella I	24	B4
Brissago CH	12	B3
Brixen/Bressanone I	14	B3
Brixlegg A	6	B1
Brno CZ	9	E4
Brolo I	34	A1
Broni I	19	E3
Bronte I	38	B3
Brouvelieures F	3	E4
Bruck an der Grossglocknerstrasse A	15	D4
Bruck an der Leitha A	9	E2
Bruck an der Mur A	16	B4
Brückl A	16	A3
Brugg CH	4	A2
Bruneck/Brúnico I	14	B3
Brúnico/Bruneck I	14	B3
Brunnen I	4	B1
Brunnen CH	4	B1
Bruyères F	3	E4
Bučany SK	9	F3
Buccheri I	38	B2
Bucchianico I	28	B3
Buchloe D	5	F3
Buchs CH	4	C2
Búcine I	24	A2
Buddusò I	22	b3
Budoni I	22	c3
Buggerru I	22	a2
Bülach CH	4	B2
Bulgnéville F	2	C4
Bulle CH	11	E4
Bultei I	22	b3
Buonalbergo I	28	C1
Buonconvento I	24	A2
Buonfornello I	37	E4
Büren CH	3	E2
Burgau D	5	E4
Burgdorf CH	3	F2
Burghausen D	7	D2
Búrgio I	36	C3
Burladingen D	4	C4
Busalla I	19	E3
Busana I	20	B1
Busca I	18	B3
Bussang F	3	E4
Busseto I	20	A3
Busto Arsízio I	12	B2
Butera I	37	E2
Buxy F	2	A2
Bzenec CZ	9	F4

C

Cabras I	22	a2
Cáccamo I	37	D4
Cadelbosco di Sopra I	20	B2
Cadenábbia I	12	C2
Cagli I	24	C2
Cágliari I	22	b1
Cagnano Varano I	29	E2
Cagnes-sur-Mer F	18	A1
Caiazzo I	28	B1
Caivano I	30	C4

Cakovec *HR*	17	D2		Cáscina *I*	23	E3		Ceresole Reale *I*	11	E2
Cala Gonone *I*	22	c3		Caselle *I*	18	B4		Cerignola *I*	29	E1
Calangiánus *I*	22	b4		Caserta *I*	30	C4		Cerknica *SLO*	15	F1
Calasetta *I*	22	a1		Casina *I*	20	B2		Černá *CZ*	7	F4
Calatafimi *I*	36	C4		Casoli *I*	28	B3		Cernay *F*	3	E3
Caldarola *I*	25	D2		Cassano delle Murge *I*	32	C4		Cernóbbio *I*	12	B2
Caldirola *I*	19	E3		Cassino *I*	28	A2		Certaldo *I*	23	F3
Calenzana *F*	22	B1		Casteggio *I*	19	E3		Cerveteri *I*	26	C3
Calitri *I*	31	E4		Castel di Sangro *I*	28	B2		Cérvia *I*	24	C4
Caltabellotta *I*	36	C3		Castel San Giovanni *I*	19	F3		Cervignano del Friuli *I*	15	D1
Caltagirone *I*	38	A2		Castel San Lorenzo *I*	31	E3		Cesana Torinese *I*	18	A4
Caltanissetta *I*	37	E3		Castel San Pietro Terme *I*	21	D1		Cesarò *I*	38	B3
Caltavuturo *I*	37	E3		Castel Volturno *I*	30	C4		Cesena *I*	24	C4
Caluso *I*	11	F1		Castelbuono *I*	37	E4		Cesenático *I*	24	C4
Calvi *F*	22	A1		Casteldelfino *I*	18	A3		České Budějovice *CZ*	8	A4
Camaiore *I*	23	E4		Castelfiorentino *I*	23	F3		České Velenice *CZ*	8	B4
Camerino *I*	25	D2		Castelfranco Emilia *I*	20	C2		Český Krumlov *CZ*	8	A4
Camigliatello *I*	35	D4		Castelfranco Véneto *I*	21	E4		Cetraro *I*	34	C4
Camogli *I*	19	E2		Castell' Arquato *I*	20	A2		Ceva *I*	18	C2
Campana *I*	35	E4		Castellabate *I*	31	D2		Ceyzériat *F*	10	B3
Campi Salentina *I*	33	E3		Castellammare del Golfo *I*	36	C4		Chabeuil *F*	10	A1
Campo Tures/Sand in Taufers *I*	14	B3		Castellammare di Stábia *I*	31	D3		Chagny *F*	2	A2
Campobasso *I*	28	C2		Castellamonte *I*	11	E1		Chalamont *F*	10	A3
Campobello di Licata *I*	37	E2		Castellana Grotte *I*	32	C4		Chalampé *F*	3	F3
Campobello di Mazara *I*	36	B3		Castellana Sicula *I*	37	E3		Challes-les-Eaux *F*	10	B2
Campocologno *CH*	13	D3		Castellaneta *I*	32	C3		Chalon-sur-Saône *F*	2	A2
Campomarino *I*	28	C2		Castellazzo Bormida *I*	19	D3		Cham *D*	4	B2
Campomarino *I*	33	D2		Castelleone *I*	19	F4		Chambéry *F*	10	B2
Campora San Giovanni *I*	35	D3		Castellina in Chiánti *I*	23	F2		Chamonix-Mont-Blanc *F*	11	D3
Camposampiero *I*	21	E4		Castellúccio dei Sáuri *I*	29	D1		Champagnole *F*	2	C1
Canazei *I*	14	B2		Castelmassa *I*	20	C3		Champéry *CH*	11	D3
Candela *I*	31	F4		Castelmauro *I*	28	C2		Champex *CH*	11	E3
Canelli *I*	18	C3		Castelnuovo della Dáunia *I*	28	C2		Champier *F*	10	A2
Canicattì *I*	37	E2		Castelnuovo di Garfagnana *I*	23	E4		Champlitte *F*	2	B3
Canicattini Bagni *I*	38	B2		Castelnuovo di Porto *I*	27	D3		Champoluc *I*	11	E2
Canino *I*	26	C4		Castelnuovo Scrívia *I*	19	E3		Chantemerle *F*	18	A4
Cánnero Riviera *I*	12	B2		Castelraimondo *I*	25	D2		Charavines *F*	10	B2
Cannes *F*	18	A1		Castelsardo *I*	22	b4		Chassigny *F*	2	B3
Canneto Sull' Óglio *I*	20	B3		Casteltérmini *I*	37	D3		Château d'Oex *CH*	11	E4
Cannóbio *I*	12	B3		Castelvecchio Subequo *I*	28	A3		Château-Queyras *F*	18	A3
Canosa di Puglia *I*	29	E1		Castelvetrano *I*	36	C3		Châteauvillain *F*	2	B4
Canossa *I*	20	B2		Castiádas *I*	22	c1		Châtel *F*	11	D3
Cantù *I*	12	C2		Castiglion Fiorentino *I*	24	B2		Châtel-St-Denis *CH*	11	D4
Cáorle *I*	21	F4		Castiglioncello *I*	23	E2		Châtillon *I*	11	E2
Cap-d'Ail *F*	18	B1		Castiglione dei Pepoli *I*	23	F4		Châtillon-sur-Chalaronne *F*	10	A3
Capaci *I*	36	C4		Castiglione del Lago *I*	24	B2		Châtillon-sur-Seine *F*	2	A4
Capistrello *I*	27	E3		Castiglione della Pescáia *I*	23	E1		Chaumergy *F*	2	B2
Capo Boi *I*	22	b1		Castiglione delle Stiviere *I*	20	B3		Chaumont *F*	2	B4
Capo Carbonara *I*	22	c1		Castiglione Messer Marino *I*	28	B2		Chaussin *F*	2	B2
Capo d'Orlando *I*	34	A1		Castrocaro Terme *I*	24	B4		Chemin *F*	2	B2
Capo di Ponte *I*	13	E2		Castroreale *I*	38	C4		Chianciano Terme *I*	24	B2
Capoliveri *I*	23	D1		Castroreale Terme *I*	34	B1		Chiaravalle *I*	35	D2
Capri *I*	30	C3		Castrovillari *I*	32	B1		Chiari *I*	13	D1
Capriati a Volturno *I*	28	B1		Catánia *I*	38	B3		Chiasso *CH*	12	B2
Capríccioli *I*	22	c4		Catanzaro *I*	35	E3		Chiavari *I*	19	E2
Capua *I*	30	C4		Catanzaro Lido *I*	35	E3		Chiavenna *I*	12	C3
Capurso *I*	32	C4		Catenanuova *I*	38	B3		Chieming *D*	6	C2
Carbónia *I*	22	a1		Cattólica *I*	24	C3		Chieri *I*	18	C4
Carbonin/Schludersbach *I*	14	C3		Cava de Tirreni *I*	31	D3		Chiesa in Valmalenco *I*	13	D3
Carcare *I*	18	C2		Cavaglià *I*	11	F1		Chieti *I*	28	B3
Cariati *I*	35	E4		Cavalese *I*	14	A2		Chióggia *I*	21	E3
Carignano *I*	18	B3		Cavárzere *I*	21	E3		Chiusa di Pesio *I*	18	B2
Carloforte *I*	22	a1		Cavo *I*	23	D1		Chiusa Sclàfani *I*	36	C3
Carmagnola *I*	18	C3		Cavour *I*	18	B3		Chiusa/Klausen *I*	14	A3
Carnia *I*	15	D2		Cazma *HR*	17	E1		Chiusaforte *I*	15	D2
Carpaneto Piacentino *I*	19	F3		Ceccano *I*	27	E2		Chiusi *I*	24	B1
Carpenédolo *I*	20	B3		Cécina *I*	23	E2		Chivasso *I*	18	C4
Carpi *I*	20	C2		Cefalù *I*	37	E4		Choye *F*	2	C3
Carpineto Romano *I*	27	E2		Ceglie Messapica *I*	33	D3		Chur *CH*	13	D4
Carpinone *I*	28	B2		Čejč *CZ*	9	E4		Cigliano *I*	11	F1
Carrara *I*	23	D4		Celano *I*	27	F3		Cingoli *I*	25	D2
Carsoli *I*	27	E3		Celerina *CH*	13	D3		Cinisi *I*	36	C4
Casacalenda *I*	28	C2		Celje *SLO*	16	B2		Cirella *I*	31	F1
Casalbuono *I*	31	F2		Celldömölk *H*	17	E4		Ciriè *I*	11	E1
Casale Monferrato *I*	19	D4		Celle Ligure *I*	19	D2		Ciró Marina *I*	35	F4
Casalecchio di Reno *I*	20	C1		Cencenighe *I*	14	B2		Cisterna di Latina *I*	27	D2
Casalmaggiore *I*	20	B3		Cento *I*	20	C2		Città della Pieve *I*	24	B1
Casalpusterlengo *I*	19	F4		Centuri *F*	22	C2		Città di Castello *I*	24	C2
Casamassima *I*	32	C4		Centúripe *I*	38	B3		Città San Angelo *I*	28	B4
Casamíccola Terme *I*	30	C3		Ceprano *I*	27	F2		Cittadella *I*	21	D4
Casamozza *F*	22	C1		Cerami *I*	38	A3		Cittaducale *I*	27	E3
Cascia *I*	27	E4		Cerchiara di Calabria *I*	32	B1		Cittanova *I*	35	D2
Casciana Terme *I*	23	E3		Cerea *I*	20	C3		Cividale di Friuli *I*	15	E2

43

Civita Castellana I	27	D3
Civitanova Marche I	25	E2
Civitavécchia I	26	C3
Civitella Roveto I	27	F2
Clairvaux-les-Lacs F	2	B1
Clavières I	18	A4
Clefmont F	2	C4
Clelles F	10	B1
Clerval CH	3	D3
Cles I	13	F3
Cluny F	2	A1
Cluses F	11	D3
Clusone I	13	D2
Codigoro I	21	E2
Codogno I	19	F4
Codróipo I	15	D1
Colfiorito I	25	D1
Colico I	12	C3
Coligny F	10	B4
Colle di Val d'Elsa I	23	F2
Colle Isarco/Gossensass I	14	A3
Collécchio I	20	B2
Colleferro I	27	E2
Collesalvetti I	23	E3
Collesano I	37	E4
Cóllio I	13	D2
Collodi I	23	E3
Collonges F	10	C3
Colmar F	3	F4
Cologna Véneta I	21	D3
Colorno I	20	B3
Colosimi I	35	D3
Comácchio I	21	E2
Combeaufontaine F	2	C3
Cómiso I	38	A2
Como I	12	B2
Conegliano I	14	C1
Conselice I	21	D1
Conselve I	21	D3
Consuma I	24	A3
Contarina I	21	E2
Contigliano I	27	D3
Contrexéville F	2	C4
Contursi Terme I	31	E3
Conversano I	32	C4
Copertino I	33	E2
Copparo I	21	D2
Corato I	32	B4
Corcieux F	3	E4
Corigliano Calabro I	32	B1
Corinaldo I	25	D3
Corleone I	36	C3
Corleto Perticara I	32	A2
Corniglio I	20	A2
Cornimont F	3	E4
Cornuda la Valle I	14	B1
Corps F	10	B1
Corréggio I	20	B2
Cortemaggiore I	20	A3
Cortemilia I	18	C3
Cortina d'Ampezzo I	14	B3
Cortona I	24	B2
Corvara in Badia I	14	B3
Cosenza I	35	D4
Cossato I	12	A2
Cossonay CH	3	D1
Couches F	2	A2
Courchevel F	10	C2
Courmayeur I	11	D2
Couvet CH	3	D2
Craco I	32	B2
Crans CH	11	E3
Crêches-sur-Saône F	10	A4
Crema I	12	C1
Crémieu F	10	A3
Cremona I	20	A3
Crescentino I	18	C4
Crespino I	21	D2
Crest F	10	A1
Cresta CH	12	C3
Crevalcore I	20	C2
Crissolo I	18	B3
Črna SLO	16	B2

Crotone I	35	F3
Cruseilles F	10	C3
Csokonyavisonta H	17	F1
Csorna H	9	F1
Cúglieri I	22	a3
Cuiseaux F	2	B1
Cuisery F	2	A1
Culoz F	10	B3
Cúneo I	18	B2
Cuorgnè I	11	E1
Cupello I	28	C3
Cutro I	35	E3

D

Dachau D	6	B3
Dačice CZ	8	C4
Dampierre F	2	C2
Dampierre-sur-Salon F	2	C3
Dannemarie F	3	E3
Darány H	17	F1
Darfo I	13	D2
Därligen CH	11	F4
Darney F	2	C4
Dasing D	6	A3
Davos CH	13	D4
Decimomannu I	22	b1
Degerndorf D	6	C2
Deggendorf D	7	D4
Delémont CH	3	E2
Délia I	37	E2
Delianuova I	34	C1
Delle F	3	E3
Denkendorf D	6	B4
Denzlingen D	4	A4
Deruta I	24	C1
Desenzano I	20	B4
Dešov CZ	8	C4
Désulo I	22	b2
Deutsch-Wagram A	9	E3
Deutschkreutz A	9	E1
Deutschlandsberg A	16	B3
Deveceser H	17	F4
Diamante I	31	F1
Diano Marina I	18	C1
Dicomano I	24	A3
Dienten A	7	D1
Diessen D	6	A2
Dietenheim D	5	E4
Dietfurt D	6	B4
Dietikon CH	4	B2
Dietmannsried D	5	E3
Dignano I	15	D2
Dijon F	2	B3
Dillingen D	5	E4
Dimaro I	13	F3
Dingli M	39	a1
Dingolfing D	6	C3
Dinozé F	3	D4
Disentis/Mustér CH	12	B4
Divonne F	10	C4
Djurdjevac HR	17	E1
Dobbiaco/Toblach I	14	C3
Dobersberg A	8	C4
Döbriach A	15	E3
Dogliani I	18	C3
Dole F	2	B2
Dolenja Vas SLO	16	A1
Dolga Vas SLO	17	D2
Dolianova I	22	b1
Döllach A	15	D3
Dolní Dvonste CZ	8	A3
Dolo I	21	E3
Dombrot-le-Sec F	2	C4
Domodóssola I	12	A3
Dompaire F	3	D4
Dómus de Maria I	22	b1
Domusnóvas I	22	a1
Domzale SLO	16	A2
Donaueschingen D	4	B3

Donaustauf D	6	C4
Donauwörth D	6	A4
Donnersbach A	15	F4
Dorfen D	6	C3
Dorgali I	22	c3
Dornauberg A	14	B4
Dornbirn A	5	D2
Dornstetten D	4	B4
Dortan F	10	B4
Doucier F	2	C1
Douvaine F	10	C4
Drachselsried D	7	D4
Drasenhofen A	9	E4
Dravograd SLO	16	B2
Drnholec CZ	9	D4
Dronero I	18	B3
Drosendorf Stadt A	8	C4
Düdingen CH	3	E1
Dugo Selo HR	17	D1
Duingt F	10	C3
Duino I	15	E1
Dunajská Streda SK	9	F2
Dürnkrut A	9	E3
Dürnstein A	8	C3

E

Eben im Pongau A	7	E1
Ebenfurth A	9	D2
Ebensee A	7	E2
Ebersberg D	6	B2
Eberschwang A	7	E2
Eberstein A	16	A3
Ebingen D	4	C4
Éboli I	31	E3
Ebreichsdorf A	9	D2
Echallens CH	3	D1
Echallon F	10	B3
Édolo I	13	E3
Eferding A	7	F3
Egervár H	17	E3
Egg A	5	D2
Eggenburg A	8	C3
Eggenfelden D	7	D3
Ehingen D	5	D4
Ehrwald A	5	F2
Eibiswald A	16	B3
Eichendorf D	7	D3
Eichstätt D	6	A4
Einsiedeln CH	4	B2
Eisenerz A	8	B1
Eisenkappel A	16	A2
Eisenstadt A	9	D2
Elbigenalp A	5	E2
Elgg CH	4	C2
Elzach D	4	A4
Emmendingen D	4	A4
Empoli I	23	F3
Endorf D	6	C2
Enese H	9	F1
Engelberg CH	4	B1
Engelhartszell A	7	E3
Engen D	4	C3
Engstingen D	4	C4
Enna I	37	E3
Enns A	8	A2
Ensisheim F	3	E3
Entlebuch CH	4	A1
Entrevaux F	18	A2
Entrèves I	11	D2
Épinal F	3	D4
Episcopía I	32	A2
Eppan/Appiano I	14	A2
Eraclea I	21	F4
Eraclea-Mare I	21	F4
Erba I	12	C2
Erbalunga F	22	C1
Ercolano I	30	C3
Erding D	6	B3
Ergoldsbach D	6	C4

Erice I	36	B4
Erlsbach A	14	C3
Ernstbrunn A	9	D3
Erstein F	4	A4
Escalaplano I	22	b2
Eschenlohe D	6	A1
Essenbach D	6	C3
Estavayer-le-Lac CH	3	D1
Este I	21	D3
Ettenheim D	4	A4
Euratsfeld A	8	B2
Evian F	11	D4
Evolène CH	11	E3

F

Faak A	15	E2
Fabriano I	25	D2
Faenza I	21	D1
Faeto I	28	C1
Faido CH	12	B3
Falcade I	14	B2
Falconara Marittima I	25	E3
Falcone I	34	B1
Fano I	25	D3
Farkasgyepü H	17	F4
Farnese I	26	C4
Fasano I	33	D3
Faucogney-et-la-Mer F	3	D4
Faulensee CH	11	F4
Favara I	37	D2
Faverges F	10	C2
Faverney F	2	C3
Fayl-Billot F	2	C4
Fehring A	17	D3
Feld A	15	E3
Feldafing D	6	A2
Feldbach A	16	C3
Feldberg D	4	A3
Feldkirch A	5	D2
Feldkirchen I	15	F3
Feldkirchen D	6	B2
Feltre I	14	B1
Fenékpuszta H	17	F3
Fener I	14	B1
Fenestrelle I	18	A4
Ferentino I	27	E2
Ferleiten A	15	D4
Fermo I	25	E2
Ferrara I	21	D2
Ferrette F	3	E3
Ferriere I	19	E3
Fertőszentmiklós H	9	E1
Fiamignano I	27	E3
Ficulle I	24	B1
Fidenza I	20	A2
Fieberbrunn A	6	C1
Fiera di Primiero I	14	B2
Fiesch CH	12	A3
Fiésole I	24	A3
Filottrano I	25	D2
Finale Emilia I	20	C2
Finale Ligure I	18	C2
Fiorenzuola d'Arda I	20	A3
Firenze I	23	F3
Firenzuola I	24	A4
Fischamend A	9	E2
Fischen D	5	E2
Fiumefreddo di Sicilia I	38	C3
Fiumicino I	26	C2
Fivizzano I	20	A1
Flaine F	11	D3
Fleurier CH	3	D2
Flims Waldhaus CH	12	C4
Floridia I	38	C2
Flüelen CH	4	B1
Flumet F	10	C2
Fluminimaggiore I	22	a2
Flums CH	4	C1
Foggia I	29	D1

Fohnsdorf A	16	A4
Foiano di Chiana I	24	B2
Folgaria I	13	F2
Foligno I	24	C1
Follónica I	23	E1
Fondi I	27	E1
Fondo I	13	F3
Fonni I	22	b2
Fontaine-Française F	2	B3
Fonyód H	17	F3
Fonzaso I	14	B2
Fóppolo I	13	D2
Fordongianus I	22	b2
Forio I	30	B3
Forlì I	24	B4
Forlì di Sannio I	28	B2
Forlimpopoli I	24	B4
Formia I	27	F1
Formigine I	20	C2
Fornaci di Barga I	23	E4
Forni di Sopra I	14	C2
Forno di Zoldo I	14	B2
Fornovo di Taro I	20	A2
Forte dei Marmi I	23	D4
Fossano I	18	B3
Fossombrone I	25	D3
Fougerolles F	3	D4
Foulain F	2	B4
Frabosa Soprana I	18	C2
Fraize F	3	E4
Francavilla al Mare I	28	B3
Francavilla di Sicilia I	38	C4
Francavilla Fontana I	33	D3
Francofonte I	38	B2
Frangy F	10	C3
Frankenburg A	7	E2
Frankenmarkt A	7	E2
Franz Josephs-Höhe A	15	D4
Frascati I	27	D2
Frasdorf D	6	C2
Frauenau D	7	E4
Frauenfeld CH	4	C3
Fregene I	26	C2
Freiburg im Breisgau D	4	A4
Freilassing D	7	D2
Freising D	6	B3
Freistadt A	8	A3
Fresnes F	2	C4
Fretigney-et-Velloreille F	2	C3
Freudenstadt D	4	B4
Freyung D	7	E4
Fribourg CH	3	E1
Frick CH	4	A3
Fridingen D	4	C3
Friedberg A	9	D1
Friedberg D	6	A3
Friedrichshafen D	5	D3
Friesach A	16	A3
Frohnleiten A	16	B4
Frontenhausen D	6	C3
Frosinone I	27	E2
Frutigen CH	11	F4
Frymburk CZ	7	F3
Fucécchio I	23	E3
Fügen A	6	B1
Fulpmes A	14	A4
Fürstenfeld A	17	D3
Fürstenfeldbruck D	6	A3
Fürstenzell D	7	E3
Furtwangen D	4	B4
Fusch A	15	D4
Füssen D	5	F2

G

Gabčíkovo SK	9	F2
Gabicce Mare I	25	D3
Gaeta I	27	F1
Gagliano del Capo I	33	F1
Gajary SK	9	E3

Galanta SK	9	F2
Galati Marina I	38	C4
Galatina I	33	E2
Galatone I	33	E2
Galeata I	24	B4
Gallarate I	12	B2
Galliate I	12	B1
Gallipoli I	33	E2
Gallneukirchen A	8	A3
Galtelli I	22	c3
Galtür A	5	E1
Gambárie I	34	C1
Gaming A	8	B2
Gammertingen D	4	C4
Gams CH	4	C2
Ganacker D	7	D4
Gandino I	13	D2
Gandria CH	12	B2
Gangi I	37	E3
Gangkofen D	6	C3
Gänserndorf A	9	E3
Garching D	6	C2
Garda I	13	E1
Gardone Riviera I	13	E1
Gardone Val Trompia I	13	D2
Garéssio I	18	C2
Gargellen A	5	D1
Gargnano I	13	E2
Garlasco I	19	E4
Garmisch Partenkirchen D	6	A1
Gars am Kamp A	8	C3
Gaschurn A	5	D1
Gasztony H	17	D3
Gattinara I	12	A2
Gavardo I	13	E1
Gavi I	19	D3
Gavoi I	22	b3
Geiselhöring D	6	C4
Geisenfeld D	6	B4
Geisenhausen D	6	C3
Geisingen D	4	B3
Gela I	37	E2
Gemona del Friuli I	15	D2
Genève CH	10	C3
Genlis F	2	B3
Génova I	19	D2
Genzano di Lucánia I	32	A3
Genzano di Roma I	27	D2
Gerace I	35	D1
Gérardmer F	3	E4
Geras A	8	C4
Geretsried D	6	B2
Gerlos A	14	B4
Gersthofen D	5	F4
Gesualdo I	31	E4
Gevrey-Chambertin F	2	A3
Gex I	10	C4
Gföhl A	8	C3
Ghedi I	20	B3
Ghilarza I	22	b3
Giardinetto I	29	D1
Giardini Naxos I	38	C3
Giarratana I	38	B2
Giarre I	38	C3
Giba I	22	a1
Gibellina Vecchia I	36	C3
Giglio Porto I	26	A4
Ginosa I	32	C3
Gióia del Colle I	32	C3
Gióia Táuro I	34	C2
Gioiosa Marea I	34	A1
Giornico CH	12	B3
Giovinazzo I	32	B4
Girifalco I	35	D3
Giromagny F	3	E3
Giulianova I	28	A4
Givry F	2	A2
Glarus CH	4	C1
Gleisdorf A	16	C4
Gletsch CH	12	A4
Gloggnitz A	9	D1
Gmünd A	15	E3
Gmünd A	8	B4

45

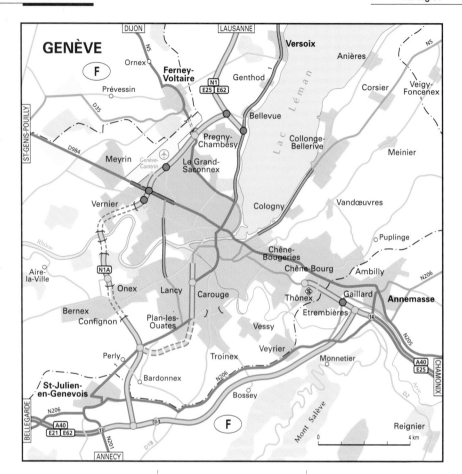

Gmund D	6	B2
Gmunden A	7	E2
Godovič SLO	15	F1
Góito I	20	B3
Golfe-Juan F	18	A1
Golfo Aranci I	22	c4
Golling A	7	D1
Goncelin F	10	B2
Gonnosfanádiga I	22	a2
Göpfritz A	8	C4
Goppenstein CH	11	F3
Gorenja Vas SLO	15	F2
Gorgonzola I	12	C1
Goričan HR	17	E2
Gorízia I	15	E1
Gornja Radgona SLO	17	D3
Gosau A	7	E1
Göschenen CH	12	B4
Gossau CH	4	C2
Gossensass/Colle Isarco I	14	A3
Gössl A	7	F1
Göstling A	8	B2
Götzis A	5	D2
Goumois CH	3	E2
Grächen CH	11	F3
Gradisca I	15	E1
Grado I	15	D1
Grafenau D	7	E4
Grafing D	6	B2
Grafrath D	6	A3
Gramatten A	8	B4
Grammichele I	38	B2
Grancey F	2	B3
Granges-sur-Vologne F	3	E4
Grassano I	32	B3
Grassau D	6	C2
Grasse F	18	A1
Gratkorn A	16	C4
Gravedona I	12	C3
Gravellona-Toce I	12	A2
Gravina in Púglia I	32	B3
Gray F	2	C3
Graz A	16	C3
Grazzanise I	30	C4
Greding D	6	B4
Greifenburg A	15	D3
Grein A	8	B3
Grenchen CH	3	E2
Grenoble F	10	B1
Gressoney-la-Trinité I	11	F2
Gressoney-St-Jean I	11	F2
Gresten A	8	B2
Greve in Chianti I	24	A3
Gries in Sellrain A	14	A4
Gries-am-Brenner A	14	A4
Griesbach D	7	D3
Grieskirchen A	7	E3
Griffen A	16	A3
Grimaldi I	35	D3
Grindelwald CH	12	A4
Grisignano di Zocco I	21	D3
Gröbming A	7	E1
Grósio I	13	E3
Gross-Gerungs A	8	B3
Gross-Siegharts A	8	C4
Grossarl A	15	D4
Grossenzersdorf A	9	E2
Grosseto I	23	F1
Grosshöchstetten CH	3	F1
Grosspetersdorf A	17	D4
Grossraming A	8	A2
Grosuplje SLO	16	A1
Grottaglie I	33	D3
Grottaminarda I	31	E4
Grottammare I	25	E1
Grotteria I	35	D2
Grubišno Polje HR	17	F1
Grünau A	7	F2
Grünburg A	7	F2
Grundlsee A	7	E1
Grüsch CH	5	D1
Gruyères CH	11	E4
Gschnitz A	14	A4
Gstaad CH	11	E4
Gstadt D	6	C2
Gsteig CH	11	E3
Gualdo Tadino I	24	C2
Guarcino I	27	E2
Guardia Sanframondi I	28	B1
Guardiagrele I	28	B3

Guasila I 22 b2
Guastalla I 20 B2
Gúbbio I 24 C2
Guebwiller F 3 E4
Guglionesi I 28 C2
Guillaumes F 18 A2
Guillestre F 18 A3
Gumpoldskirchen A 9 D2
Gundelfingen D 5 E4
Gunten CH 3 F1
Günzburg D 5 E4
Gurk A 15 F3
Gurtnellen CH 12 B4
Gúspini I 22 a2
Güssing A 17 D3
Gutenstein A 8 C2
Guttannen CH 12 A4
Gwatt CH 3 F1
Gy F 2 C3
Györ H 9 F1

H

Haag A 8 A2
Haag D 6 C3
Haag am Hausruck A 7 E2
Haar D 6 B2
Hahót H 17 E3
Haigerloch D 4 C4
Hainburg A 9 E2
Hainfeld A 8 C2
Halámky CZ 8 B4
Haldensee A 5 E2
Hall in Tirol A 14 B4
Hallein A 7 D1
Hallstatt A 7 E1
Handegg CH 12 A4
Hardegg A 8 C4
Hartberg A 17 D4
Haslach A 7 F3
Haslach D 4 B4
Haté CZ 9 D4
Haugsdorf A 9 D3
Haunersdorf D 7 D3
Hausach D 4 B4
Häusern D 4 B3
Hausham D 6 B2
Haut-Asco F 22 B1
Haute-Nendaz CH 11 E3
Hechingen D 4 C4
Hegyeshalom H 9 F2
Hegyhátsál H 17 E3
Heidenreichstein A 8 B4
Heiligenberg D 4 C3
Heiligenblut A 15 D4
Heiligenkreuz A 17 D3
Heimertingen D 5 E3
Heiterwang A 5 F2
Hemau D 6 B4
Hengersberg D 7 D4
Herbertingen D 5 D3
Hergiswil CH 4 B1
Héricourt F 3 D3
Herisau CH 4 C2
Hermagor A 15 E3
Herrsching D 6 A2
Herzogenburg A 8 C3
Hévíz H 17 F3
Hevlin CZ 9 D4
Heyrieux F 10 A2
Hieflau A 8 B1
Hilterfingen CH 3 F1
Hindelang D 5 E2
Hinterrhein CH 12 C3
Hinterstoder A 7 F1
Hinterthal A 7 D1
Hintertux A 14 B4
Hinterzarten D 4 A3
Hirschegg A 5 E2
Hirsingue F 3 E3

Hluboká nad Vltavou CZ 8 A4
Hluk CZ 9 F4
Hochburg A 7 D2
Hochdorf CH 4 B2
Höchenschwand D 4 B3
Hodonín CZ 9 E4
Hodoš SLO 17 D3
Hodošan HR 17 E2
Hohenau A 9 E3
Hohenberg A 8 C2
Hohenbrunn D 6 B2
Hohenems A 5 D2
Höhenkirchen D 6 B2
Hohenlinden D 6 B3
Hohenpeissenberg D 5 F3
Hohenschwangau D 5 F2
Hohentauern A 8 A1
Holíč SK 9 F4
Hollabrunn A 9 D3
HolLád H 17 F3
Holmec SLO 16 B2
Holzgau A 5 E2
Holzkirchen D 6 B2
Hopfgarten A 6 C1
Horb D 4 C4
Horgen CH 4 B2
Horitschon A 9 E1
Horn A 8 C3
Horn D 4 C3
Hornberg D 4 B4
Horní Planá CZ 7 F4
Horní Vltavice CZ 7 E4
Horw CH 4 B1
Hospental CH 12 B4
Hrádek CZ 9 D4
Hrotovice CZ 9 D4
Hrušovany CZ 9 D4
Huben A 14 C3
Hüfingen D 4 B3
Husinec CZ 7 F4
Hustopeče CZ 9 F4
Hüttschlag A 15 D4
Huttwil CH 3 F2

I

Ichenhausen D 5 E4
Idrija SLO 15 F1
Idro I 13 E2
Igea Marina I 24 C4
Iglesias I 22 a1
Igls A 14 A4
Iharosberény H 17 E2
Ilanz CH 12 C4
Illertissen D 5 E4
Illmitz A 9 E1
Immenstaad D 4 C3
Immenstadt D 5 E2
Imola I 21 D1
Imperia I 18 C1
Imst A 5 F2
Incisa in Val d'Arno I 24 A3
Ingolstadt D 6 B4
Innertkirchen CH 12 A4
Innichen/San Candido I 14 C3
Inning D 6 A2
Innsbruck A 14 A4
Ins CH 3 E2
Interlaken CH 11 F4
Intra I 12 B2
Inzell D 7 D2
Iolanda di Savóia I 21 D1
Irdning A 7 F1
Irsina I 32 B3
Is-sur-Tille F 2 C2
Ischgl A 5 E1
Ischia I 30 C3
Iselle I 12 A3
Iselsberg A 15 D3
Iseo I 13 D2

Isernia I 28 B2
Ísili I 22 b2
Ismaning D 6 B3
Isny D 5 D3
Isola F 18 A2
Isola 2000 F 18 A2
Isola del Liri I 27 F2
Isola della Scala I 20 C3
Ísola di Capo Rizzuto I 35 F3
Íspica I 38 B1
Itri I 27 F1
Íttiri I 22 b3
Ivančice CZ 9 D4
Ivanič Grad HR 17 D1
Ivanska HR 17 E1
Ivréa I 11 F1
Izernore F 10 B3

Jablonica SK 9 F3
Jánosháza H 17 F4
Jánossomorja H 9 E2
Jaroměřice nad Rokytnou CZ 8 C4
Jastrebarsko HR 16 C1
Jaun CH 11 E4
Jausiers F 18 A3
Jelsi I 28 C2
Jemnice CZ 8 C4
Jenbach A 6 B1
Jennersdorf A 17 D3
Jerzu I 22 c2
Jesenice A 15 F2
Jesi I 25 D2
Jésolo I 21 F4
Jevišovice CZ 9 D4
Jezersko SLO 16 A2
Jindřichův Hradec CZ 8 B4
Jougne F 3 D1
Juan-les-Pins F 18 A1
Judenburg A 16 A4
Jussey F 2 C4

Kadarküt H 17 F2
Kaindorf A 16 C4
Kaisheim D 6 A4
Kalce SLO 15 F1
Kals A 14 C3
Kalsdorf A 16 C3
Kalwang A 8 B1
Kám H 17 E3
Kamnik SLO 16 A2
Kandern D 3 F3
Kandersteg CH 11 F4
Kapfenberg A 8 B1
Kaplice CZ 8 A4
Kaprun A 15 D4
Kapuvar H 9 E1
Kardašova-Řečice CZ 8 B4
Karlstift A 8 B3
Kaufbeuren D 5 E3
Kaufering D 5 F3
Kauns A 5 E1
Kaysersberg F 3 E4
Kefermarkt A 8 A3
Kelheim D 6 B4
Kemenny Újezd CZ 8 A4
Kempten D 5 E3
Kenzingen D 4 A4
Kerzers CH 3 E2
Keszthely H 17 F3
Kiefersfelden D 6 C1
Kiental CH 11 F4
Kindberg A 8 C1
Kirchbach A 16 C3

Kirchberg A	6	C1
Kirchberg an der Pielach A	8	C2
Kirchdorf an der Krems A	7	F2
Kirchschlag A	9	D1
Kisslegg D	5	D3
Kittsee A	9	E2
Kitzbühel A	6	C1
Klagenfurt A	15	F3
Klaus an der Pyhrnbahn A	7	F2
Klausen/Chiusa I	14	A3
Kleinhaugsdorf A	9	D4
Klinča Selo HR	16	C1
Klingenbach A	9	E1
Kloštar HR	17	F1
Klösterle A	5	D1
Klosterneuburg A	9	D3
Klosters CH	13	D4
Knittelfeld A	16	B4
Kobarid SLO	15	E2
Kochel D	6	A2
Köflach A	16	B3
Kolbermoor D	6	C2
Königsbrunn D	5	F4
Königsfeld D	4	B4
Königssee D	7	D1
Königswiesen A	8	B3
Köniz CH	3	E1
Konstanz D	4	C3
Kópháza H	9	E1
Koprivnica HR	17	E2
Körmend H	17	E3
Korneuburg A	9	D3
Korpavár H	17	E3
Koryčany CZ	9	F4
Kössen A	6	C2
Kőszeg H	17	E4
Kötschach-Mauthen A	15	D3
Kranj SLO	15	F2
Kranjska Gora SLO	15	E2
Krapina HR	16	C2
Krauchenwies D	4	C3
Krems A	8	C3
Kremsmünster A	7	F2
Kreuth D	6	B1
Kreuzlingen CH	4	C3
Krieglach A	8	C1
Krimml A	14	C4
Križevci HR	17	D1
Krško SLO	16	C1
Krumbach D	5	E4
Krumpendorf A	15	F3
Krün D	6	A1
Küblis CH	5	D1
Kuchl A	7	D1
Kufstein A	6	C1
Kühtai A	5	F2
Kumrovec HR	16	C1
Kunovice CZ	9	F4
Kunžak CZ	8	B4
Küssnacht CH	4	B2
Kúty SK	9	E3
Kyjov CZ	9	E4

L

L'Alpe-d'Huez F	10	B1
L'Aquila I	27	F3
L'Argentiére-la-Bessée F	18	A3
L'Echalp F	18	A3
L'Escarène F	18	B1
L'Isle-sur-le-Doubs F	3	D3
L'Ile-Rousse I	22	B1
La Bérarde F	10	C1
La Bresse F	3	E4
La Caletta I	22	c3
La Chambre F	10	C2
La Chapelle F	10	A4
La Chapelle-en-Vercors F	10	A1
La Chaux-de-Fonds CH	3	D2
La Clusaz F	10	C3

La Cluse F	10	B3
La Cluse-et-Mijoux F	3	D2
La Côte-St-André F	10	A2
La Cure F	10	C4
La Grave F	10	C1
La Lima I	23	E4
La Maddalena I	22	c4
La Mure F	10	B1
La Napoule-Plage F	18	A1
La Neuveville CH	3	E2
La Plagne F	11	D2
La Punt CH	13	D3
La Roche-sur-Foron F	10	C3
La Rochette F	10	C2
La Spézia I	19	F1
La Thuile I	11	D2
La Tour-du-Pin F	10	B2
La Turbie F	18	B1
Laa an der Thaya A	9	D3
Lábod H	17	F2
Lacco Ameno I	30	C3
Lacedonia I	31	E4
Lacona I	23	D1
Láconi I	22	b2
Ladispoli I	26	C3
Laferté F	2	C4
Laffrey F	10	B1
Lagnieu F	10	B3
Lagonegro I	31	F2
Lahr D	4	A4
Laichingen D	5	D4
Laignes F	2	A4
Laiguéglia I	18	C1
Laimbach A	8	B3
Lama di Peligni I	28	B3
Lamarche F	2	C4
Lambach A	7	E2
Lamprechtshausen A	7	D2
Lana I	13	F3
Lanciano I	28	B3
Landau D	7	D4
Landeck A	5	E1
Landquart CH	5	D1
Landsberg D	5	F3
Landshut D	6	C3
Langen A	5	D1
Langenargen D	5	D2
Längenfeld A	5	F1
Langenisarhofen D	7	D4
Langenlois A	8	C3
Langenthal CH	3	F2
Langenwang A	8	C1
Langhirano I	20	B2
Langnau im Emmental CH	3	F1
Languaid D	6	C4
Langres F	2	B4
Langweid D	5	F4
Lanslebourg-Mont-Cenis F	11	D1
Lantosque F	18	B2
Lanusei I	22	c2
Lanžhot CZ	9	E3
Lanzo Torinese I	11	E1
Lapoutroie F	3	E4
Larche F	18	A3
Larderello I	23	E2
Lari F	22	C2
Larino I	28	C2
Laško SLO	16	B2
Lastra a Signa I	23	F3
Laterza I	32	C3
Latiano I	33	D3
Latina I	27	E1
Latisana I	21	F4
Latronico I	32	A2
Laufen CH	4	A3
Laufen D	7	D2
Laufenburg CH	4	A3
Laufenburg D	4	A3
Lauingen D	5	E4
Laupen CH	3	E1
Laupheim D	5	D4
Laurenzana I	32	A3
Lauria I	31	F2

Lausanne CH	11	D4
Lauterbrunnen CH	11	F4
Lavagna I	19	E2
Lavamünd A	16	B3
Lavarone I	14	A1
Lavello I	31	F4
Lavinio-Lido di Enea I	27	D2
Lavis I	13	F2
Lazise I	20	C4
Le Bar F	18	A1
Le Bourg d'Oisans F	10	B1
Le Bourget F	10	B2
Le Châtelard F	10	C2
Le Locle CH	3	D2
Le Markstein F	3	E4
Le Monêtier-les-Bains F	10	C1
Le Pont-de-Beauvoisin F	10	B2
Le Pont-de-Claix F	10	B1
Le Russey F	3	D2
Le Thillot F	3	E4
Le Touvet F	10	B2
Le Trayas F	18	A1
Lecce I	33	E2
Lecco I	12	C2
Lech A	5	E2
Lechovice CZ	9	D4
Legnago I	20	C3
Legnano I	12	B2
Lehnice SK	9	F2
Leibnitz A	16	C3
Leipheim D	5	E4
Leissigen CH	11	F4
Lenart SLO	16	C2
Lend A	15	D4
Lendava SLO	17	D2
Lendinara I	21	D3
Lenggries D	6	B2
Lengyeltóti H	17	F3
Lenk CH	11	E4
Lenna I	13	D2
Lenno I	12	C2
Lenora CZ	7	E4
Lenti H	17	E3
Lenting D	6	B4
Lentini I	38	B2
Lenzburg CH	4	A2
Lenzerheide CH	13	D4
Lenzkirch D	4	B3
Leoben A	16	B4
Leogang A	7	D1
Leonforte I	37	F3
Leopoldsdorf A	9	E2
Lepoglava HR	17	D2
Lercara Friddi I	37	D3
Lerici I	19	F1
Lermoos A	5	F2
Les Abrets F	10	B2
Les Adrets F	18	A1
Les Arcs F	11	D2
Les Contamines-Montjoie F	11	D2
Les Deux-Alpes F	10	C1
Les Diablerets CH	11	E3
Les Echelles F	10	B2
Les Gets F	11	D3
Les Haudères CH	11	E3
Les Houches F	11	D3
Les Laumes F	2	A3
Les Menuires F	10	C1
Les Planches-en-Montagne F	2	C1
Les Riceys F	2	A4
Les Rousses F	10	C4
Les Trois-Epis F	3	E4
Lesa I	12	B2
Lesina I	29	D2
Letenye H	17	E2
Leuglay F	2	A4
Leuk CH	11	E3
Leukerbad CH	11	E3
Leutasch A	6	A1
Leutkirch D	5	D3
Leutschach A	16	C3
Lévanto I	19	F2
Levens F	18	A1

Levico Terme *I* 14 A2
Levier *F* 2 C2
Leysin *CH* 11 D3
Licata *I* 37 E2
Lido degli Estensi *I* 21 E2
Lido di Camaiore *I* 23 D3
Lido di Castel Fusano *I* 27 D2
Lido di Jésolo *I* 21 F3
Lido di Latina *I* 27 D1
Lido di Metaponto *I* 32 C2
Lido di Nazioni *I* 21 E2
Lido di Ostia *I* 26 C2
Lido di Pomposa *I* 21 E2
Lido di Spina *I* 21 E2
Lido di Torre Mileto *I* 29 D2
Lido di Venézia *I* 21 E3
Lido Silvana *I* 33 D2
Lienz *A* 15 D3
Liestal *CH* 3 F3
Liezen *A* 7 F1
Lignano Pineta *I* 15 D1
Lignano Sabbiadoro *I* 15 D1
Lilienfeld *A* 8 C2
Limone Piemonte *I* 18 B2
Limone sul Garda *I* 13 E2
Limonest *F* 10 A3
Lindau *D* 5 D2
Lindenberg *D* 5 D2
Linderhof *D* 5 F2
Linguaglossa *I* 38 C3
Linthal *CH* 4 C1
Linz *A* 8 A3
Lioni *I* 31 E4
Lipica *SLO* 15 E1
Lipno *CZ* 7 F3
Lišov *CZ* 8 A4
Litija *SLO* 16 B1
Livigno *I* 13 D3
Livorno *I* 23 D3
Ljubelj *SLO* 15 F2
Ljubljana *SLO* 16 A1
Ljubno *SLO* 16 B2
Ljutomer *SLO* 17 D2
Loano *I* 18 C2
Locarno *CH* 12 B3
Lockenhaus *A* 17 D4
Locorotondo *I* 33 D3
Locri *I* 35 D1
Lodè *I* 22 c3
Lodi *I* 19 F4
Lofer *A* 7 D1
Logatec *SLO* 15 F1
Loiano *I* 20 C1
Lóiri *I* 22 c4
Lomello *I* 19 D4
Lomnice nad Lužnici *CZ* 8 B4
Lonato *I* 20 B4
Lončarica *HR* 17 F1
Longarone *I* 14 C2
Longeau *F* 2 B4
Longobucco *I* 35 E4
Lonigo *I* 21 D3
Lons-le-Saunier *F* 2 B1
Loosdorf *A* 8 C2
Loreo *I* 21 E3
Loreto *I* 25 E2
Loreto Aprutino *I* 28 A3
Lorica *I* 35 D3
Lörrach *D* 3 F3
Losenstein *A* 8 A2
Lossburg *D* 4 B4
Lotzorai *I* 22 c2
Louhans *F* 2 B1
Lovére *I* 13 D2
Lövö *H* 9 E1
Lož *SLO* 16 A1
Lozzo di Cadore *I* 14 C2
Lucca *I* 23 E3
Lucera *I* 29 D1
Lucito *I* 28 C2
Ludbreg *HR* 17 E2
Ludwigshafen *D* 4 C3
Lugagnano Val d'Arda *I* 19 F3

Lugano *CH* 12 B2
Lugo *I* 21 D1
Luino *I* 12 B2
Lukovica *SLO* 16 A2
Lungern *CH* 4 A1
Lungro *I* 32 A1
Lunz *A* 8 B2
Luogosanto *I* 22 b4
Lupoglav *HR* 17 D1
Lure *F* 3 D3
Lustenau *A* 5 D2
Lutzmannsburg *A* 9 E1
Luxeuil-les-Bains *F* 3 D3
Luzern *CH* 4 B2
Luzzara *I* 20 B3
Lyon *F* 10 A3
Lyss *CH* 3 E2

M

Macerata *I* 25 E2
Macerata Féltria *I* 24 C3
Macomer *I* 22 b3
Mâcon *F* 10 A4
Macugnaga *I* 11 F2
Maddaloni *I* 30 C4
Madésimo *I* 12 C3
Madonna di Campíglio *I* 13 E3
Magenta *I* 12 B1
Magione *I* 24 B2
Magliano dei Marsi *I* 27 E3
Magliano in Toscana *I* 26 B4
Magliano Sabina *I* 27 D3
Maglie *I* 33 E2
Maîche *F* 3 D2
Maida *I* 35 D3
Maienfeld *CH* 5 D1
Mainburg *D* 6 B4
Maiori *I* 31 D3
Maisach *D* 6 A3
Maissau *A* 8 C3
Malacky *SK* 9 E3
Malbuisson *F* 2 C1
Malcésine *I* 13 E2
Malé *I* 13 F3
Mallersdorf *D* 6 C4
Málles Venosta/Mals im Vinschgau *I* 13 E4
Mallnitz *A* 15 D3
Malo *I* 21 D4
Maloja *CH* 13 D3
Mals im Vinschgau/Málles Venosta *I* 13 E4
Mammola *I* 35 D2
Manching *D* 6 B4
Manciano *I* 26 B4
Mándas *I* 22 b2
Mandelieu *F* 18 A1
Manduria *I* 33 D2
Manérbio *I* 20 B3
Manfredónia *I* 29 E2
Maniago *I* 14 C2
Mank *A* 8 C2
Mantova *I* 20 C3
Maranello *I* 20 C2
Marano Lagunare *I* 15 D1
Maratea *I* 31 F2
Marboz *H* 10 B4
Marcali *H* 17 F2
Marchaux *F* 2 C3
Marchegg *A* 9 E3
Marciana Marina *I* 23 D1
Marckolsheim *F* 3 F4
Margherita di Savoia *I* 29 E1
Maria Taferl *A* 8 B2
Maria Wörth *A* 15 F3
Mariazell *A* 8 C2
Maribor *SLO* 16 C2
Marina di Árbus *I* 22 a2
Marina di Campo *I* 23 D1
Marina di Caronía *I* 38 A4
Marina di Carrara *I* 23 D4

Marina di Castagneto-Donorático *I* 23 E2
Marina di Chiéuti *I* 29 D2
Marina di Gáiro *I* 22 c2
Marina di Ginosa *I* 32 C3
Marina di Gioiosa Jónica *I* 35 D1
Marina di Grosseto *I* 23 E1
Marina di Léuca *I* 33 F1
Marina di Massa *I* 23 D4
Marina di Pietrasanta *I* 23 D4
Marina di Pisa *I* 23 D3
Marina di Ragusa *I* 38 A1
Marina di Ravenna *I* 21 E1
Marina di San Vito *I* 28 B3
Marina Romea *I* 21 E1
Marinadi Torre Grande *I* 22 a2
Marinella *I* 36 C3
Marineo *I* 37 D4
Maristella *I* 22 a3
Markdorf *D* 4 C3
Markt St Florian *A* 8 A2
Markt St Martin *A* 9 D1
Markt-Indersdorf *D* 6 B3
Marktl *D* 7 D3
Marktoberdorf *D* 5 E3
Marnay *F* 2 C3
Maróstica *I* 14 B1
Marotta *I* 25 D3
Marquartstein *D* 6 C2
Marradi *I* 24 B4
Marsala *I* 36 B3
Marsciano *I* 24 C1
Marsico Nuovo *I* 31 F3
Marta *I* 26 C4
Martano *I* 33 E2
Martigny *CH* 11 D3
Martina Franca *I* 33 D3
Martina/Martinsbruck *CH* 13 E4
Martinsbruck/Martina *CH* 13 E4
Mártis *I* 22 b4
Masevaux *F* 3 E3
Massa *I* 23 D4
Massa Marittima *I* 23 E2
Massafra *I* 32 C3
Matelica *I* 25 D2
Matera *I* 32 B3
Mathay *F* 3 D3
Matrei am Brenner *A* 14 A4
Matrei in Osttirol *A* 14 C3
Mattersburg *A* 9 D1
Mattighofen *A* 7 D2
Mattinata *I* 29 E2
Mattsee *A* 7 D2
Mauerkirchen *A* 7 D3
Mautern *A* 8 B1
Mauterndorf *A* 15 E4
Mauth *D* 7 E4
Mauthausen *A* 8 A3
Mauvoisin *CH* 11 E3
Mayrhofen *A* 14 B4
Mazara del Vallo *I* 36 B3
Mazzarino *I* 37 E2
Mazzaró *I* 38 C3
Meckenbeuren *D* 5 D3
Mede *I* 19 D4
Medicina *I* 21 D1
Medved'ov *SK* 9 F2
Medvode *SLO* 16 A2
Meersburg *D* 4 C3
Megève *F* 11 D3
Meilen *CH* 4 B2
Meina *I* 12 B2
Meiringen *CH* 12 A4
Meitingen *D* 5 F4
Mel *I* 14 B2
Meldola *I* 24 B4
Melegnano *I* 12 C1
Melfi *I* 31 F4
Melilli *I* 38 B2
Mélisey *F* 3 D3
Melito di Porto Salvo *I* 39 D4
Melk *A* 8 C2
Mellieha *M* 39 a2
Memmingen *D* 5 E3

49

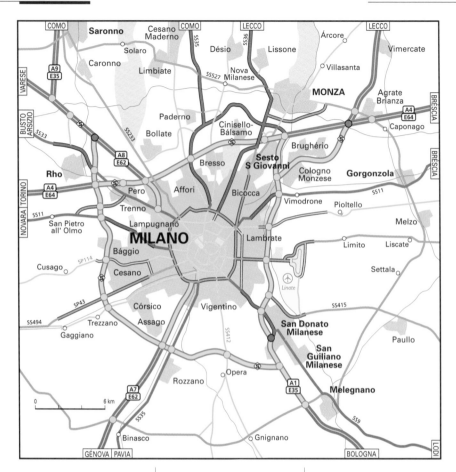

Menággio I	12	C2
Menfi I	36	C3
Ménfőcsanak H	9	F1
Mengen D	4	C3
Mengeš SLO	16	A2
Mens F	10	B1
Menthon F	10	C3
Menton F	18	B1
Meran/Merano I	13	F3
Merano/Meran I	13	F3
Mercatale I	24	B2
Mercatino Conca I	24	C3
Mercato San Severino I	31	D3
Mercato Saraceno I	24	C4
Méribel F	10	C2
Mering D	5	F4
Merklingen D	5	D4
Merligen CH	11	F4
Mervans F	2	B2
Mesagne I	33	E3
Mesocco CH	12	C3
Mésola I	21	E2
Messina I	34	C1
Messkirch D	4	C3
Messtetten D	4	C4
Mestre I	21	E3
Metabief F	2	C1
Metlika SLO	16	B1
Metnitz A	15	F3
Metten D	7	D4

Metzingen D	4	C4
Meximieux F	10	A3
Meyzieu F	10	A3
Mezzolombardo I	13	F3
Mgarr M	39	a2
Micheldorf A	7	F2
Mieders A	14	A4
Miesbach D	6	B2
Migliarino I	21	D2
Miglionico I	32	B3
Mijoux F	10	C4
Mikulov CZ	9	E4
Milano I	12	C1
Milano Marittima I	24	C4
Milazzo I	34	B1
Mileto I	35	D2
Millstatt A	15	E3
Mindelheim D	5	E3
Minervino Murge I	32	A4
Minturno I	27	F1
Mira I	21	E3
Miramar F	18	A1
Miramare I	24	C4
Mirándola I	20	C2
Mirebeau F	2	B3
Misilmeri I	37	D4
Missanello I	32	A2
Mistelbach A	9	E3
Misterbianco I	38	B3
Mistretta I	37	F4

Misurina I	14	C3
Mittelberg A	5	E2
Mittelberg A	5	F1
Mittelberg D	5	E2
Mittenwald D	6	A1
Mittersill A	14	C4
Modane F	11	D1
Módena I	20	C2
Módica I	38	B1
Modigliana I	24	B4
Mödling A	9	D2
Modra SK	9	F3
Modugno I	32	C4
Moena I	14	B2
Móglia I	20	C2
Moirans F	10	B2
Moirans-en-Montagne F	10	B4
Mola di Bari I	32	C4
Molare I	19	D3
Molfetta I	32	B4
Molinella I	21	D2
Moliterno I	32	A2
Möllbrücke A	15	E3
Moloy F	2	A3
Molveno I	13	F2
Monaco MC	18	B1
Monasterace Marina I	35	E2
Monastir I	22	b1
Moncalieri I	18	C4
Mönchdorf A	8	B3

Mönchhof A 9 E2
Mondello I 37 D4
Mondolfo I 25 D3
Mondovi I 18 C2
Mondragone I 30 C4
Mondsee A 7 E2
Monéglia I 19 E2
Monestier-de-Clermont F 10 B1
Monfalcone I 15 E1
Monguelfo/Welsberg I 14 B3
Monheim D 6 A4
Mönichkirchen A 9 D1
Monopoli I 33 D4
Monreale I 37 D4
Monsélice I 21 D3
Monsummano Terme I 23 E3
Mont-sous-Vaudrey F 2 B2
Montagnana I 21 D3
Montalcino I 24 A2
Montalto del Marche I 25 E1
Montalto di Castro I 26 B3
Montana CH 11 E3
Montbard F 2 A4
Montbéliard F 3 D3
Montbenoît F 3 D2
Montbonnot F 10 B1
Monte San Savino I 24 B2
Monte Sant'Angelo I 29 E2
Monte-Carlo MC 18 B1
Montebelluna I 14 B1
Montecatini-Terme I 23 E3
Montécchio I 25 D3
Montécchio Maggiore I 21 D4
Montecorvino Rovella I 31 E3
Montefalco I 24 C1
Montefiascone I 26 C4
Montefiorino I 20 B1
Montegiordano Marina I 32 B2
Montegrotto Terme I 21 D3
Montella I 31 E3
Montenero di Bisaccia I 28 C2
Montepulciano I 24 B2
Montereale I 27 E4
Monterotondo I 27 D3
Montesano sulla Marcellana I .. 31 F2
Montesarchio I 31 D4
Montescaglioso I 32 B3
Montesilvano Marina I 28 B4
Montevarchi I 24 A3
Montgenèvre F 18 A4
Monthey CH 11 D3
Monthureaux-sur-Saône F 2 C4
Monti I 22 c4
Montichiari I 20 B3
Monticiano I 23 F2
Montigny-le-Roi F 2 C4
Montigny-sur-Aube F 2 A4
Montluel F 10 A3
Montmélian F 10 C2
Montmirey F 2 B2
Montorio al Vomano I 27 F4
Montpont-en-Bresse F 2 A1
Montret F 2 A1
Montreux CH 11 D4
Montrevel F 10 A4
Monza I 12 C1
Moosburg D 6 B3
Moosinning D 6 B3
Morano Cálabro I 32 A1
Moravské Budějovice CZ 8 C4
Moravský Krumlov CZ 9 D4
Morbegno I 12 C3
Mörbisch A 9 E1
Morciano di Romagna I 24 C3
Morcone I 28 C1
Morcote CH 12 B2
Móres I 22 b3
Morestel F 10 B2
Moretta I 18 B3
Morez F 10 C4
Morges CH 11 D4
Morgex I 11 D2
Morgins CH 11 D3

Mori I 13 F2
Mormanno I 32 A1
Morosaglia F 22 B1
Mortara I 19 D4
Morteau F 3 D2
Morzine F 11 D3
Moschendorf A 17 D3
Mosonmagyaróvár H 9 F2
Mössingen D 4 C4
Mosta M 39 b1
Motta di Livenza I 21 F4
Mottola I 32 C3
Mouchard F 2 C2
Moudon CH 3 D1
Mougins F 18 A1
Mouthe F 2 C1
Mouthier F 2 C2
Moutier CH 3 E2
Moûtiers F 10 C2
Muccia I 25 D1
Mühlbach A 15 D4
Mühldorf D 6 C3
Mulhouse F 3 E3
Müllheim D 3 F3
München D 6 B3
Münsingen CH 3 F1
Münsingen D 5 D4
Münster CH 12 A3
Munster F 3 E4
Münstertal D 4 A3
Münzkirchen A 7 E3
Murano I 21 E3
Murato F 22 C1
Murau A 15 F4
Muravera I 22 c1
Mureck A 16 C3
Muri CH 4 B2
Murnau D 6 A2
Muro Calenzana F 22 B1
Muro Lucano I 31 E3
Mürren CH 11 F4
Murska Sobota SLO 17 D3
Mursko Središče HR 17 D2
Murten CH 3 E1
Mürzsteg A 8 C1
Mürzzuschlag A 8 C1
Mussomeli I 37 D3
Mussy F 2 A4
Müstair CH 13 E3
Muster/Disentis CH 12 B4
Myjava SK 9 F4

N

Näfels CH 4 C2
Nagyatád H 17 F2
Nagybajom H 17 F2
Nagycenk H 9 E1
Nagygyimót H 17 F4
Nagykanizsa H 17 E2
Nagyvázsony H 17 F3
Nantua F 10 B3
Napoli I 30 C4
Narbolia I 22 a3
Narcao I 22 a1
Nardo I 33 E2
Narni I 27 D4
Naro I 37 D2
Narta HR 17 E1
Naso I 34 A1
Nassereith A 5 F2
Naturno/Naturns I 13 F3
Naturns/Naturno I 13 F3
Nauders A 13 E4
Navelli I 28 A3
Navilly F 2 B2
Nedelišće HR 17 D2
Nendeln FL 5 D2
Nepi I 27 D3
Nersingen D 5 E4

Nervi I 19 E2
Nesselwang D 5 E2
Netolice CZ 7 F4
Nettuno I 27 D2
Neuburg D 6 A4
Neuchâtel CH 3 E2
Neuenburg D 3 F3
Neuf-Brisach F 3 F4
Neufahrn D 6 C4
Neufelden A 7 F3
Neuhaus D 7 E3
Neuhausen am Rheinfall CH 4 B3
Neuhofen an der Krems A 7 F2
Neuilly-l'Évêque F 2 B4
Neukirchen A 14 C4
Neulengbach A 8 C2
Neumarkt A 7 D2
Neumarkt A 16 A4
Neumarkt-St Veit D 6 C3
Neunagelberg A 8 B4
Neunkirchen A 9 D1
Neuötting D 7 D3
Neupölla A 8 C3
Neusiedl am See A 9 E2
Neustadt D 4 B3
Neustadt D 6 B4
Neustift A 14 A4
Neuville F 10 A3
Nicastro I 35 D3
Nice F 18 A1
Nickelsdorf A 9 E2
Nicolosi I 38 B3
Nicosia I 37 F3
Nieder Stotzingen D 5 E4
Niederalteich D 7 D4
Niederau A 6 C1
Niederwinkling D 7 D4
Nittendorf D 6 C4
Nizza Monferrato I 19 D3
Nocera I 31 D3
Nocera Umbra I 24 C2
Noceto I 20 A2
Noci I 32 C3
Noépoli I 32 B2
Nogara I 20 C3
Nogent F 2 B4
Nola I 31 D4
Nolay F 2 A2
Noli I 18 C2
Nomexy F 3 D4
Nonnenhorn D 5 D2
Nonza F 22 C1
Norcia I 25 D1
Noto I 38 B1
Nova H 17 E3
Nová Bystřice CZ 8 B4
Nova Gorica SLO 15 E1
Nova Levante/Welschnofen I 14 A2
Novaféltria I 24 C3
Novara I 12 B1
Novara di Sicilia I 38 C4
Nové Hrady CZ 8 B4
Novellara I 20 B2
Noventa Vicentina I 21 D3
Novi di Módena I 20 C2
Novi Ligure I 19 D3
Novi Marof HR 17 D2
Novigrad Podravski HR 17 E1
Novo Mesto SLO 16 B1
Nozeroy F 2 C1
Nuits-St-Georges F 2 A2
Nulvi I 22 b4
Numana I 25 E2
Nuoro I 22 c3
Nurallao I 22 b2
Nyon CH 10 C4

O

Oberammergau D 6 A1

51

Oberau D	6	A1
Oberaudorf D	6	C1
Oberdrauburg A	15	D3
Obergrafendorf A	8	C2
Obergünzburg D	5	E3
Obergurgl A	13	F4
Oberhofen CH	3	F1
Oberjoch D	5	E2
Obernberg A	7	E3
Oberndorf A	7	D2
Oberndorf D	4	B4
Obernzell D	7	E3
Oberpullendorf A	9	D1
Oberriet CH	5	D2
Oberstaufen D	5	D2
Oberstdorf D	5	E2
Obertauern A	15	E4
Obertraubling D	6	C4
Obertraun A	7	E1
Obervellach A	15	D3
Oberwald CH	12	A4
Oberwart A	17	D4
Oberwölz A	15	F4
Oberzeiring A	16	A4
Obing D	6	C2
Öblarn A	7	F1
Obsteig A	5	F2
Occhiobello I	21	D2
Ochsenhausen D	5	D3
Odelzhausen D	6	A3
Oderzo I	21	F4
Oetz A	5	F2
Ogliastro Cilento I	31	E2
Ólbia I	22	c4
Oléggio I	12	B2
Oletta F	22	C1
Oliena I	22	c3
Olivone CH	12	B3
Olmedo I	22	a3
Olten CH	4	A2
Omegna I	12	A2
Opicina I	15	E1
Oppido Lucano I	32	A3
Oppido Mamertina I	34	C1
Ora/Auer I	14	A2
Orani I	22	b3
Orbassano I	18	B4
Orbe CH	3	D1
Orbetello I	26	B4
Orbey F	3	E4
Orgelet F	2	B1
Orgosolo I	22	b3
Oria I	33	D3
Oriolo I	32	B2
Oristano I	22	a2
Öriszentpéter H	17	D3
Ormea I	18	C2
Ormož SLO	17	D2
Ornans F	2	C2
Oron-la-Ville CH	11	D4
Orosei I	22	c3
Orsières CH	11	E3
Orsogna I	28	B3
Ort A	7	E3
Orta Nova I	29	D1
Orta s Giúlio I	12	A2
Orte I	27	D4
Ortenburg D	7	D3
Orth A	9	E2
Ortisei/St Ulrich I	14	B3
Ortona I	28	B3
Ortueri I	22	b2
Orvieto I	24	B1
Orvinio I	27	E3
Orzinuovi I	20	A4
Óschiri I	22	b3
Ósilo I	22	b4
Osimo I	25	E2
Ospedaletti I	18	B1
Ossiach A	15	F3
Osterhofen D	7	D4
Ostiglia I	20	C3
Ostra I	25	D3
Ostrach D	5	D3
Ostuni I	33	D3
Osztopán H	17	F2
Otočec SLO	16	B1
Otranto I	33	F2
Ottana I	22	b3
Ottaviano I	31	D3
Ottenschlag A	8	B3
Ottensheim A	7	F3
Öttevény H	9	F1
Ottobeuren D	5	E3
Ottone I	19	E3
Oulx I	18	A4
Ovada I	19	D3
Ovidoli I	27	F3
Oyonnax F	10	B4
Ožbalt SLO	16	C2
Ozieri I	22	b3

P

Paceco I	36	B4
Pachino I	38	B1
Pacsa H	17	E3
Padova I	21	D3
Padru I	22	c3
Paesana I	18	B3
Paestum I	31	E3
Paladru F	10	B2
Palagiano I	32	C3
Palagonia I	38	B2
Palau I	22	c4
Palazzo San Gervasio I	32	A4
Palazzolo I	13	D1
Palazzolo Acréide I	38	B2
Palena I	28	B3
Palermo I	37	D4
Palestrina I	27	E2
Palinuro I	31	E2
Palma di Montechiaro I	37	D2
Palmadula I	22	a4
Palmanova I	15	D1
Palmi I	34	C2
Palo del Colle I	32	B4
Palombara Sabina I	27	D3
Paluzza I	15	D2
Pamhagen A	9	E1
Pandino I	12	C1
Pantelleria	36	A1
Paola I	35	D4
Pápa H	17	F4
Papasidero I	32	A1
Pappenheim D	6	A4
Parabita I	33	E2
Parma I	20	B2
Parpan CH	13	D4
Partanna I	36	C3
Partenen A	5	D1
Partinico I	36	C4
Passau D	7	E3
Passignano sul Trasimeno I	24	B2
Patergassen A	15	E3
Paternion A	15	E3
Paternò I	38	B3
Paternopoli I	31	E4
Patersdorf D	7	D4
Patsch A	14	A4
Pattada I	22	b3
Pavia I	19	E4
Pavullo nel Frignano I	20	C1
Payerne CH	3	D1
Pedráces/Pedratsches I	14	B3
Pedratsches/Pedráces I	14	B3
Peggau A	16	C4
Pegli I	19	D2
Peio I	13	E3
Peira-Cava F	18	B2
Peiss D	6	B2
Peissenberg D	6	A2
Peiting D	5	F3
Pellegrino Parmense I	20	A2
Pennabilli I	24	C3
Penne I	28	A4
Penzberg D	6	A2
Perchtoldsdorf A	9	D2
Perg A	8	A3
Pérgine Valsugana I	14	A2
Pergola I	25	D3
Pernitz A	9	D2
Pérouges F	10	A3
Persenbeug A	8	B2
Pertisau A	6	B1
Perúgia I	24	C2
Pésaro I	25	D3
Pescara I	28	B4
Pescasseroli I	28	A2
Peschici I	29	E2
Peschiera del Garda I	20	B4
Péscia I	23	E3
Pescina I	27	F3
Pescocostanzo I	28	B2
Pescolanciano I	28	B2
Pescopagano I	31	E3
Pesmes F	2	B3
Petilia Policastro I	35	E3
Petralia I	37	E3
Petrella Tifernina I	28	C2
Pettenbach A	7	F2
Peuerbach A	7	E3
Pezinok SK	9	F3
Pfaffenhausen D	5	E4
Pfaffenhofen D	6	B3
Pfaffikon CH	4	B2
Pfäffikon CH	4	B2
Pfafflar A	5	E2
Pfarrkirchen D	7	D3
Pfatter D	6	C4
Pfeffenhausen D	6	B4
Pfronten D	5	E2
Pfullendorf D	4	C3
Pfullingen D	4	C4
Pfunds A	5	E1
Philippsreut D	7	E4
Piacenza I	19	F3
Piádena I	20	B3
Piana Crixia I	18	C2
Piana degli Albanesi I	37	D4
Pianoro I	20	C1
Piazza Armerina I	37	F2
Piazza al Serchio I	20	B1
Picerno I	31	F3
Pico I	27	F1
Piediluco I	27	D4
Piedimonte Matese I	28	B1
Pienza I	24	B2
Pierre-de-Bresse F	2	B2
Pietra Ligure I	18	C2
Pietraperzia I	37	E3
Pietrasanta I	23	D4
Pieve di Cadore I	14	C2
Pieve di Teco I	18	C2
Pieve San Stéfano I	24	B3
Pievepelago I	20	B1
Pinerolo I	18	B3
Pineto I	28	B4
Pinkafeld A	17	D4
Pino F	22	C2
Pinzolo I	13	E2
Pióbbico I	24	C3
Piombino I	23	E1
Piotta CH	12	B3
Piove di Sacco I	21	E3
Piovene-Rocchette I	14	A1
Pisa I	23	E3
Pisciotta I	31	E2
Pisogne I	13	D2
Pisticci I	32	B2
Pistóia I	23	F3
Pitigliano I	26	B4
Pitomača HR	17	F1
Pivka SLO	15	F1
Pivnica HR	17	F1
Pizzo I	35	D2

Pizzoli I 27 E4
Planina SLO 15 F1
Plansee A 5 F2
Platamona Lido I 22 a4
Plati I 35 D1
Plattling D 7 D4
Ploaghe I 22 b3
Plombierès-sur-Bains F 3 D4
Pöchlarn A 8 B2
Pocking D 7 E3
Podersdorf am See A 9 E2
Podivín CZ 9 E4
Podkoren SLO 15 E2
Podravska Slatina HR 17 F1
Poggibonsi I 23 F2
Póggio Rusco I 20 C3
Pohořelice CZ 9 D4
Poirino I 18 C3
Polesella I 21 D2
Policastro I 31 E2
Policoro I 32 B2
Polignano a Mare I 32 C4
Poligny F 2 B2
Polistena I 35 D2
Pomarance I 23 E2
Pomézia I 27 D2
Pompaples CH 3 D1
Pompei I 31 D3
Pomposa I 21 E2
Poncin F 10 B3
Ponsacco I 23 E3
Pont-d'Ain F 10 B3
Pont-de-Roide F 3 D3
Pont-de-Vaux F 10 A4
Pont-en-Royans F 10 A1
Pont-St-Martin I 11 F2
Pontailler-sur-Saône F 2 B3
Pontarlier F 3 D2
Pontassieve I 24 A3
Pontcharra F 10 B2
Ponte Arche I 13 F2
Ponte della Venturina I 23 F4
Ponte di Legno I 13 E3
Ponte di Piave I 21 E4
Ponte nelle Alpi I 14 C2
Ponte Tresa CH 12 B2
Ponte-Leccia F 22 B1
Pontebba I 15 D2
Pontedecimo I 19 D2
Pontedera I 23 E3
Pontelandolfo I 28 C1
Pontelongo I 21 E3
Pontevico I 20 A3
Pontremoli I 19 F2
Pontresina CH 13 D3
Popoli I 28 A3
Poppi I 24 B3
Populónia I 23 E2
Pordenone I 14 C1
Pörnbach D 6 B4
Porrentruy CH 3 E3
Porretta Terme I 23 F4
Port-sur-Saône F 2 C3
Porto Azzurro I 23 D1
Porto Cervo I 22 c4
Porto Cesareo I 33 E2
Porto Corsini I 21 E1
Porto d'Áscoli I 25 E1
Porto Empedocle I 37 D2
Porto Ércole I 26 B4
Porto Garibaldi I 21 E2
Porto Rotondo I 22 c4
Porto San Giorgio I 25 E2
Porto Santo Stéfano I 26 A4
Porto Tolle I 21 E2
Porto Tórres I 22 a4
Portoferráio I 23 D1
Portofino I 19 E2
Portomaggiore I 21 D2
Portoscuso I 22 a1
Portovenere I 19 F1
Pörtschach A 15 F3
Posada I 22 c3

Poschiavo CH 13 D3
Positano I 31 D3
Posta I 27 E4
Postojna SLO 15 F1
Potenza I 31 F3
Potrogruaro I 21 F4
Pottenstein A 9 D2
Pöttmes D 6 A4
Pouilly-en-Auxois F 2 A3
Poysdorf A 9 E3
Pozzallo I 38 B1
Pozzomaggiore I 22 b3
Pozzuoli I 30 C3
Prachatice CZ 7 F4
Prägraten A 14 C4
Praia a Mare I 31 F1
Praiano I 31 D3
Pralognan-la-Vanoise F 11 D2
Pratella I 28 B1
Prato I 23 F3
Prauthoy F 2 B3
Pravlov CZ 9 D4
Pré St-Didier I 11 D2
Predappio I 24 B4
Predazzo I 14 B2
Preddvor SLO 16 A2
Predel SLO 15 E2
Predlitz A 15 E4
Predoi/Prettau I 14 C4
Pregarten A 8 A3
Pressbaum A 9 D2
Prettau/Predoi I 14 C4
Prien D 6 C2
Primolano I 14 B1
Priverno I 27 E2
Prizzi I 37 D3
Prunn D 6 B4
Ptuj SLO 16 C2
Puchberg A 8 C2
Puget-Théniers F 18 A2
Pula I 22 b1
Pulkau A 8 C3
Punta Ala I 23 E1
Punta Marina I 21 E1
Purbach A 9 E2
Purgstall A 8 B2
Purkersdorf A 9 D2
Putignano I 32 C3

Q

Quartu S Elena I 22 b1
Quingey F 2 C2

R

Raab A 7 E3
Raabs an der Thaya A 8 C4
Rábafüzes H 17 D3
Rabat M 39 a1
Rača SK 9 E2
Racconigi I 18 B3
Radeče SLO 16 B1
Radenci SLO 17 D3
Radenthein A 15 E3
Radkersburg A 17 D3
Radlje ob Dràvi SLO 16 B3
Radmirje SLO 16 B2
Radolfzell D 4 C3
Radošovce SK 9 F4
Radovljica SLO 15 F2
Radstadt A 7 E1
Raffadali I 37 D3
Ragaška Slatina SLO 16 C2
Ragusa I 38 B1
Rain D 6 A4
Rajka H 9 F2

Ramacca I 38 B2
Ramsau A 7 E1
Ranalt A 14 A4
Randazzo I 38 B3
Rankweil A 5 D2
Rapallo I 19 E2
Rapolla I 31 F4
Rapperswil CH 4 B2
Raron CH 11 F3
Rastenfeld A 8 C3
Ratece SLO 15 E2
Ratten A 8 C1
Rattenberg A 6 B1
Rattersdorf A 17 D4
Raubling D 6 C2
Rauris A 15 D4
Ravanusa I 37 E2
Ravello I 31 D3
Ravenna I 21 E1
Ravensburg D 5 D3
Razdrto SLO 15 F1
Realp CH 12 B4
Recanati I 25 E2
Recey-sur-Ource F 2 A4
Rechnitz A 17 D4
Recoaro Terme I 13 F1
Recologne F 2 C2
Rédics H 17 D2
Regalbuto I 38 B3
Regen D 7 D4
Regensburg D 6 C4
Reggello I 24 A3
Réggio di Calàbria I 39 D4
Réggio Nell 'Emilia I 20 B2
Reggiolo I 20 C2
Reichenau an der Rax A 8 C1
Reichertshausen D 6 B3
Reichertshofen D 6 B4
Reignier F 10 C3
Reinach CH 3 F3
Reinach CH 4 A2
Reisbach D 7 D3
Reischach D 7 D3
Reischenhart D 6 C2
Reit im Winkl D 6 C2
Rejštejn CZ 7 E4
Remiremont F 3 D4
Rennweg A 15 E3
Répcelak H 17 E4
Resana I 21 E4
Retz A 9 D4
Reutlingen D 4 C4
Reutte A 5 F2
Revfülöp H 17 F3
Rheinfelden CH 3 F3
Rheinfelden D 3 F3
Rhinau F 4 A4
Rho I 12 B1
Riale I 12 B3
Ribeauville F 3 F4
Ribera I 36 C3
Ribnica SLO 16 A1
Riccia I 28 C1
Riccione I 24 C3
Ried A 5 E1
Ried im Innkreis A 7 E3
Riedenburg D 6 B4
Riedlingen D 5 D4
Riegel D 4 A4
Riegersburg A 17 D3
Riesi I 37 E2
Rieti I 27 E1
Riezlern A 5 E2
Rimini I 24 C4
Rimske Toplice SLO 16 B1
Riomaggiore I 19 F1
Rionero in Vulture I 31 F4
Rioz F 2 C3
Ripatransone I 25 E1
Riposto I 38 C3
Riquewihr F 3 F4
Riva I 13 D2
Rivarolo Canavese I 11 E1

53

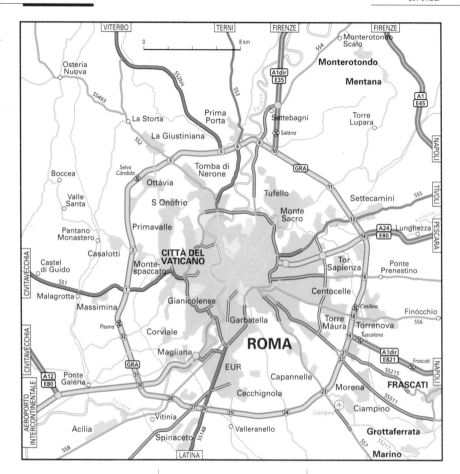

Rivoli *I*	18	B4
Rocca di Mezzo *I*	27	F3
Rocca San Casciano *I*	24	B4
Roccadáspide *I*	31	E3
Roccalbegna *I*	24	A1
Roccalumera *I*	38	C4
Roccamonfina *I*	28	A1
Roccapalumba *I*	37	D3
Roccaraso *I*	28	B2
Roccastrada *I*	23	F2
Roccella Jónica *I*	35	D2
Rochefort-s-Nenon *F*	2	B2
Rodi Gargánico *I*	29	E2
Rogatec *SLO*	16	C2
Rogliano *F*	22	C2
Rogliano *I*	35	D3
Rohrbach *A*	7	F3
Rolle *CH*	10	C4
Roma *I*	27	D2
Romagnano Sésia *I*	12	A2
Romans-sur-Isère *F*	10	A1
Romanshorn *CH*	4	C2
Romont *CH*	3	D1
Roncegno *I*	14	A2
Ronchamp *F*	3	D3
Ronchi *I*	15	E1
Ronciglione *I*	26	C3
Roquebillière *F*	18	B2
Roquebrune-Cap-Martin *F*	18	B1
Rorschach *CH*	5	D2

Rosarno *I*	34	C2
Rosegg *A*	15	F3
Rosenheim *D*	6	C2
Roseto degli Abruzzi *I*	28	B4
Rosice *CZ*	9	D4
Rosignano-Maríttimo *I*	23	E2
Rosolina Mare *I*	21	E3
Rosolini *I*	38	B1
Rossano *I*	35	E4
Rosshaupten *D*	5	F2
Rotondella *I*	32	B2
Rott *D*	5	F3
Rott *D*	6	C2
Rottach *D*	6	B2
Rottenburg *D*	4	C4
Rottenburg *D*	6	C4
Rottenmann *A*	8	A1
Rotthalmünster *D*	7	D3
Rottweil *D*	4	B4
Rouffach *F*	3	E4
Rougemont *F*	3	D3
Rougemont *F*	3	E3
Rovato *I*	13	D1
Rovereto *I*	13	F2
Rovigo *I*	21	D3
Rovisče *HR*	17	E1
Roybon *F*	10	A2
Rubiera *I*	20	B2
Ruffieux *F*	10	B3
Ruhmannsfelden *D*	7	D4

Ruhpolding *D*	6	C2
Rum *H*	17	E4
Rumilly *F*	10	C3
Rupt *F*	3	D4
Russi *I*	21	E1
Rust *A*	9	E2
Rust *D*	4	A4
Ruswil *CH*	4	A2
Rüti *CH*	4	B2
Rutigliano *I*	32	C4
Ruvo di Puglia *I*	32	B4

S

Saal *D*	6	B4
Saalbach *A*	6	C1
Saales *F*	3	E4
Saalfelden *A*	7	D1
Saanen *CH*	11	E4
Saas-Fee *CH*	11	F3
Sabáudia *I*	27	E1
Sabbioneta *I*	20	B3
Sacile *I*	14	C1
Saignelégier *CH*	3	E2
St Aegyd *A*	8	C2
St-Amé *F*	3	D4
St-Amour *F*	10	B4

St Andrä A	16	B3
St Anton A	5	E1
St Blasien D	4	A3
St-Cergue CH	10	C4
St Christina/Santa Cristina I	14	B3
St Christoph A	5	E1
St-Claude F	10	C4
St-Dié F	3	E4
St-Donat-sur-l'Herbasse F	10	A1
St Englmar D	7	D4
St-Etienne-de-St-Geoirs F	10	A2
St Etienne-de-Tinée F	18	A2
St-Florent F	22	C1
St Gallen A	8	A1
St Gallen CH	4	C2
St Gallenkirch A	5	D1
St-Genix-sur-Guiers F	10	B2
St Georgen A	7	E2
St Georgen A	16	A4
St Georgen D	4	B4
St-Germain-de-Joux F	10	B3
St-Germain-du-Bois F	2	B2
St-Germain-du-Plain F	2	A1
St-Gervais-les-Bains F	11	D3
St Gilgen A	7	E2
St Gingolph CH	11	D4
St-Gorgon-Main F	3	D2
St-Hippolyte F	3	D2
St-Imier CH	3	E2
St Jakob im Rosental A	15	F2
St-Jean-Cap-Ferrat F	18	B1
St-Jean-de-Bournay F	10	A2
St-Jean-de-Losne F	2	B2
St-Jean-de-Maurienne F	10	C1
St-Jeoire F	10	C3
St Johann am Tauern A	16	A4
St Johann im Pongau A	15	D4
St Johann in Tirol A	6	C1
St-Jorioz F	10	C3
St-Julien-en-Genevois F	10	C3
St Lambrecht A	15	F4
St-Laurent-en-Grandvaux F	2	C1
St Leonhard A	8	B2
St Lorenzen A	15	D3
St-Louis F	3	F3
St-Loup-sur-Semouse F	3	D4
St Luc CH	11	E3
St-Marcellin F	10	A1
St Märgen D	4	A4
St-Martin-Vésubie F	18	A2
St-Maurice CH	11	D3
St Maurice-sur-Moselle F	3	E3
St Michael A	15	E4
St Michael A	16	B4
St Michael A	17	D4
St-Michel-de-Maurienne F	10	C1
St Moritz CH	13	D3
St Niklaus I	11	F3
St Nikolai I	15	F4
St Oswald A	8	A3
St Paul A	16	B3
St-Paul F	18	A3
St-Paul F	18	A1
St-Pierre-d'Albigny F	10	C2
St-Pierre-de-Chartreuse F	10	B2
St Pölten A	8	C2
St-Rambert-en-Bugey F	10	B3
St-Sauveur-sur-Tinée F	18	A2
St-Seine-l'Abbaye F	2	A3
St-Symphorien-d'Ozon F	10	A2
St-Thiébault F	2	C4
St-Trivier-de-Courtes F	10	A4
St Ulrich/Ortisei I	14	B3
St Valentin A	8	A2
St-Vallier-de-Thiey F	18	A1
St Veit A	15	D3
St-Véran F	18	A3
St Vigil/San Vigilio I	14	B3
St Vincent I	11	E2
St Wolfgang A	7	E2
Ste-Croix CH	3	D1
Ste-Marie-aux-Mines F	3	E4
Sala Consilina I	31	F3
Sale I	19	D3
Salem D	4	C3
Salemi I	36	C3
Salerno I	31	D3
Saline di Volterra I	23	E2
Salins F	2	C2
Sallanches F	11	D3
Salò I	13	E1
Salsomaggiore Terme I	20	A2
Saluzzo I	18	B3
Salzburg A	7	D2
Salzweg D	7	E3
Samassi I	22	b2
Sambuca di Sicilia I	36	C3
Samedan CH	13	D3
Sambor HR	16	C1
Samoëns F	11	D3
Šamorín SK	9	F2
Samugheo I	22	b2
San Antioco I	22	a1
San António di Gallura I	22	c4
San Bartolomeo in Galdo I	28	C1
San Benedetto del Tronto I	25	E1
San Benedetto in Alpe I	24	B4
San Benedetto Po I	20	C3
San Bernardino CH	12	C3
San Biágio Plátani I	37	D3
San Bonifacio I	20	C3
San Candido/Innichen I	14	C3
San Casciano in Val di Pesa I	23	F3
San Cataldo I	37	E3
San Cataldo I	33	E2
San Cipirello I	36	C4
San Daniele del Friuli I	15	D2
San Donaci I	33	E3
San Felice Circeo I	27	E1
San Felice sul Panaro I	20	C2
San Ferdinando di Puglia I	29	E1
San Fratello I	38	B4
San Gavino Monreale I	22	b2
San Germano I	12	A1
San Gimignano I	23	F2
San Giórgio di Nogaro I	15	D1
San Giorgio Iónico I	33	D3
San Giovanni a Piro I	31	E2
San Giovanni di Sinis I	22	a2
San Giovanni in Fiore I	35	E3
San Giovanni in Persiceto I	20	C2
San Giovanni Rotondo I	29	E2
San Giovanni Suergiu I	22	a1
San Giovanni Valdarno I	24	A3
San Giovanni-in-Croce I	20	B3
San Giuliano Terme I	23	E3
San Giustino I	24	B3
San Leonardo in Passiria I	14	A3
San Lorenzo Nuovo I	26	C4
San Lucido I	35	D4
San Marcello Pistoiese I	23	E4
San Marco dei Cavoti I	28	C1
San Marco in Lamis I	29	D2
San Marino RSM	24	C3
San Martino di Castrozza I	14	B2
San Michele all'Ádige I	13	F3
San Miniato I	23	E3
San Nicolò I	21	D2
San Nicolò Gerrei I	22	b2
San Pancrazio Salentino I	33	E3
San Pellegrino Terme I	12	C2
San Piero a Sieve I	24	A3
San Pietro in Casale I	21	D2
San Pietro Vernotico I	33	E3
San Polo d'Enza I	20	B2
San Quirico d'Orcia I	24	A2
San Remo I	18	B1
San Rufo I	31	E3
San Severino Marche I	25	D2
San Severo I	29	D2
San Sosti I	32	A1
San Stéfano di Cadore I	14	C3
San Stéfano Quisquina I	37	D3
San Stino di Livenza I	21	F4
San Valentino alla Muta I	13	E4
San Vigilio/St Vigil I	14	B3
San Vincenzo I	23	E2
San Vito I	22	c1
San Vito al Tagliamento I	15	D1
San Vito dei Normanni I	33	D3
San Vito di Cadore I	14	C2
San Vito lo Capo I	36	B4
Sand in Taufers/Campo Tures I	14	B3
Sandl A	8	A3
Sandrigo I	21	D4
Sanluri I	22	b2
Sannazzaro de 'Burgondi I	19	E4
Sannenmöser CH	11	E4
Sannicandro di Bari I	32	C4
Sannicandro Gargánico I	29	D2
Sansepolcro I	24	B3
Sant' Ágata Militello I	38	B4
Sant' Andrea di Conza I	31	E3
Sant' Andrea Frius I	22	b2
Sant' Ángelo in Vado I	24	C3
Sant' Angelo Lodigiano I	19	E4
Sant' Elia a Pianist I	28	C2
Sant' Eufémia Lamézia I	35	D3
Santa Caterina di Pittinuri I	22	a3
Santa Caterina Valfurva I	13	E3
Santa Caterina Villarmosa I	37	E3
Santa CesZrea I	33	F2
Santa Cristina/St Christina I	14	B3
Santa Croce di Magliano I	28	C2
Santa Dona' di Piave I	21	F4
Santa Lucia del Mela I	34	B1
Santa Margherita I	22	b1
Santa Margherita di Bélice I	36	C3
Santa Margherita Ligure I	19	E2
Santa Maria Cápua Vetere I	30	C4
Santa Maria Maggiore I	12	B3
Santa Maria Navarrese I	22	c2
Santa Marinella I	26	C3
Santa Ninfa I	36	C3
Santa Severa F	22	C1
Santa Severa I	26	C3
Santa Sofia I	24	B3
Santa Teresa di Riva I	38	C4
Santa Teresa Gallura I	22	b4
Santarcángelo di Romagna I	24	C4
Santena I	18	C4
Santeramo in Colle I	32	C3
Santhià I	11	F1
Santo Stefano di Camastra I	37	F4
Santu Lussúrgiu I	22	b3
Santuário di Oropa I	11	F2
Sappada I	14	C3
Sapri I	31	F2
Sárdara I	22	b2
Sarentino-Sarntal I	14	A3
Sargans CH	4	C1
Sarnano I	25	D1
Sarnen CH	4	A1
Sárnico I	13	D2
Sarno I	31	D3
Saronno I	12	B2
Sarroch I	22	b1
Sársina I	24	B3
Sárvár H	17	E4
Sarzana I	23	D4
Sassari I	22	b4
Sassenage F	10	B1
Sasso Marconi I	20	C1
Sassoferrato I	25	D2
Sassuolo I	20	B2
Šaštin- Stráže SK	9	E3
Sauerlach D	6	B2
Saulgau D	5	D3
Saulx F	3	D3
Saulxures F	3	E4
Sauze d'Oulx I	18	A4
Savelletri I	33	D3
Savelli I	35	E4
Savigliano I	18	B3
Savignano Irpino I	29	D1
Savignano sul Rubicone I	24	C4
Savognin CH	13	D3
Savona I	19	D2
Scafa I	28	A3

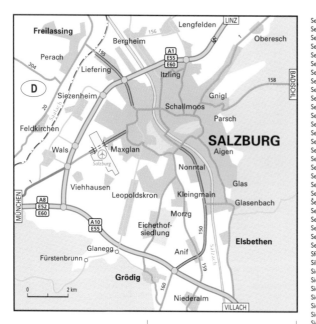

Freilassing
Bergheim
Perach
Liefering
Siezenheim
Feldkirchen
Wals
Maxglan
Viehhausen
Leopoldskron
Glanegg
Fürstenbrunn
Grödig
Lengfelden
Oberesch
Itzling
Gnigl
Schallmoos
Parsch
SALZBURG
Aigen
Nonntal
Kleingmain
Morzg
Eichethof-siedlung
Anif
Niederalm
Glas
Glasenbach
Elsbethen
LINZ
BAD/SCHL
MÜNCHEN
VILLACH
0   2 km

Serfaus A	5	EI
Seriate I	13	D2
Sermide I	20	C3
Serra San Bruno I	35	D2
Serracapriola I	29	D2
Serradifalco I	37	E3
Sersale I	35	E3
Servigliano I	25	EI
Sessa Aurunca I	28	AI
Sesto Calende I	12	B2
Sesto Fiorentino I	23	F3
Sesto/Sexten I	14	C3
Sestola I	20	BI
Sestri Levante I	19	E2
Sestriere I	18	A4
Sesvete HR	17	DI
Settebagni I	27	D3
Settimo Torinese I	18	C4
Seui I	22	b2
Seulo I	22	b2
Seurre F	2	B2
Ševětín CZ	8	A4
Sevnica SLO	16	BI
Sevrier F	10	C3
Sexten/Sesto I	14	C3
Seyssel F	10	B3
Sežana SLO	15	EI
Sforzacosta I	25	E2
Sibari I	32	BI
Siderno I	35	DI
Siegenburg D	6	B4
Sieggraben A	9	DI
Siegsdorf D	6	C2
Siena I	24	A2
Sierentz F	3	F3
Sierning A	8	A2
Sierre CH	11	E3
Sigmaringen D	4	C4
Silandro/Schlanders I	13	F3
Silánus I	22	b3
Siliqua I	22	b1
Sillian A	14	C3
Sils-Maria CH	13	D3
Silvaplana CH	13	D3
Silvi Marina I	28	B4
Silz A	5	F2
Simaság H	17	E4
Simaxis I	22	b2
Simbach D	7	D3
Simbach D	7	D3
Simmerberg D	5	D2
Simplon Dorf CH	11	F3
Sinalunga I	24	B2
Singen D	4	C3
Siniscola I	22	c3
Sinopoli I	34	CI
Sion CH	11	E3
Siracusa I	38	C2
Sirmione I	20	B4
Sirnach CH	4	C2
Sirolo I	25	E2
Sissach CH	4	A2
Sistiana I	15	EI
Siusi I	14	A3
Skalica SK	9	F4
Škofja Loka SLO	15	F2
Škofljica SLO	16	AI
Sládkovičovo SK	9	F2
Slatina HR	16	CI
Slavonice CZ	8	C4
Sliema M	39	b1
Slovenj Gradec SLO	16	B2
Slovenska Bistrica SLO	16	C2
Slovenske Konjice SLO	16	C2
Sluderno/Schluderns I	13	E4
Smědeč CZ	7	F4
Soave I	20	C3
Sobotište SK	9	F3
Sodražica SLO	16	AI
Solda/Sulden I	13	E3
Sölden A	5	FI
Söll A	6	CI
Sollenau A	9	D2

Scalea I	31	FI	Schwanenstadt A	7	E2
Scandiano I	20	B2	Schwarzach A	15	D4
Scanno I	28	A2	Schwarzsee CH	11	E4
Scansano I	23	FI	Schwaz A	6	BI
Scanzano Iónico I	32	B2	Schwechat A	9	D2
Scardovari I	21	E2	Schwenningen D	4	B4
Schaan FL	5	D2	Schwyz CH	4	BI
Schachendorf A	17	D4	Sciacca I	36	C3
Schaffhausen CH	4	B3	Scicli I	38	BI
Schäftlam D	6	B2	Scilla I	34	CI
Schärding A	7	E3	Scorze I	21	E4
Scharnitz A	6	AI	Scuol CH	13	E4
Scharnstein A	7	F2	Seckau A	16	B4
Scheer D	4	C4	Sédico I	14	B2
Schéggia I	24	C2	Sédilo I	22	b3
Scheibbs A	8	B2	Sédini I	22	b4
Scheifling A	16	A4	Sedrun CH	12	B4
Scheyern D	6	B3	Seeboden A	15	E3
Schierling D	6	C4	Seebruck D	6	C2
Schilpário I	13	D2	Seefeld in Tyrol A	6	AI
Schiltach D	4	B4	Seelbach D	4	A4
Schio I	21	D4	Seeon D	6	C2
Schladming A	7	EI	Seeshaupt D	6	A2
Schlanders/Silandro I	13	F3	Seewalchen A	7	E2
Schleching D	6	C2	Seewiesen A	8	BI
Schliersee D	6	B2	Segesd H	17	F2
Schluchsee D	4	B3	Seitenstetten A	8	A2
Schluderns/Sluderno I	13	E4	Sélestat F	3	F4
Schludersbach/Carbonin I	14	C3	Sellières F	2	B2
Schöder A	15	F4	Selongey F	2	B3
Schönau D	4	A3	Selva di Val Gardena/		
Schönberg A	14	A4	Wolkenstein in Gardena I	14	B3
Schönberg A	7	E4	Selvino I	13	D2
Schongau D	5	F3	Semmering A	8	CI
Schönwald D	4	B4	Senec SK	9	F2
Schopfheim D	4	A3	Senica SK	9	F3
Schoppernau A	5	D2	Senigállia I	25	D3
Schramberg D	4	B4	Senise I	32	B2
Schrems A	8	B4	Sennecey-le-Grand F	2	AI
Schrobenhausen D	6	A3	Sénnori I	22	b4
Schröcken A	5	D2	Senorbi I	22	b2
Schruns A	5	DI	Senožeče SLO	15	FI
Schüpfheim CH	4	AI	Sentilj SLO	16	C3
Schwabhausen D	6	A3	Seravezza I	23	D4
Schwabmünchen D	5	F4	Sered' SK	9	F3
Schwanden CH	4	CI	Seregno I	12	C2

Sološnica SK	9	F3
Solothurn CH	3	F2
Solvay I	23	E2
Sombernon F	2	A3
Sommatino I	37	E2
Somogyszob H	17	F2
Sonceboz CH	3	E2
Soncino I	20	A4
Sóndalo I	13	E3
Sondrio I	13	D3
Sonogno CH	12	B3
Sonthofen D	5	E2
Sopron H	9	E1
Sora I	27	F2
Soragna I	20	A3
Soresina I	20	A3
Sórgono I	22	b2
Soriano nel Cimino I	26	C4
Sorrento I	30	C3
Sorso I	22	b4
Sortino I	38	B2
Sospel F	18	B1
Sottomarina I	21	E3
Soultz F	3	E3
Soverato I	35	D2
Soveria Mannelli I	35	D3
Spaichingen D	4	C4
Sparta I	34	C1
Spello I	24	C1
Sperlonga I	27	E1
Spezzano Albanese I	32	B1
Spiegelau D	7	E4
Spielfeld A	16	C3
Spiez CH	11	F4
Spilimbergo I	15	D2
Spinazzola I	32	A4
Špišić Bukovica HR	17	F1
Spital am Pyhrn A	8	A1
Spittal an der Drau A	15	E3
Spitz A	8	C3
Splügen CH	12	C3
Spoleto I	24	C1
Spotorno I	19	D2
Spresiano I	14	C1
Squinzano I	33	E3
Stachy CZ	7	E4
Stainach A	7	F1
Stainz A	16	B3
Stalden CH	11	F3
Stams A	5	F2
Stans CH	4	B1
Stansstad CH	4	B1
Staré Město CZ	9	F4
Stari Gradac HR	17	F1
Starnberg D	6	A2
Stechelberg CH	11	F4
Steckborn CH	4	C3
Steeg A	5	F2
Stegersbach A	17	D4
Stein am Rhein CH	4	C3
Steinach A	14	A4
Steinfeld A	15	D3
Steingaden D	5	F3
Steinhausen D	5	D3
Sterzing/Vipiteno I	14	A3
Steyr A	8	A2
Steyrermühl A	7	E2
Stia I	24	B3
Stigliano I	32	B3
Stilo I	35	D2
Stintino I	22	a4
Štitary CZ	8	C4
Stockach D	4	C3
Stockerau A	9	D3
Storo I	13	E2
Strà I	21	E3
Stradella I	19	E4
Stráni CZ	9	F4
Stranice SLO	16	B2
Strassburg A	16	A3
Strasswalchen A	7	D2
Straubing D	6	C4
Strážnice CZ	9	F4
Strážný CZ	7	E4
Strengberg A	8	A2
Stresa I	12	B2
Strmilov CZ	8	B4
Strobl A	7	E2
Strongoli I	35	E3
Stuben A	5	E1
Studánky CZ	8	A3
Studená CZ	8	C4
Stühlingen D	4	B3
Stupava SK	9	E3
Stupnik HR	16	C1
Suaredda I	22	c3
Subbiano I	24	B3
Subiaco I	27	E2
Suchdol nad Lužnicí CZ	8	B4
Sulden/Solda I	13	E3
Sulmona I	28	A3
Sulz D	4	B4
Sümeg H	17	F3
Sumiswald CH	3	F2
Suni I	22	a3
Sursee CH	4	A2
Susa I	18	A4
Susch CH	13	D4
Sutri I	26	C3
Suzzara I	20	B3
Svätý Jur SK	9	F3
Szany H	9	F1
Szil H	9	F1
Szombathely H	17	E4

T

Taggia I	18	B1
Tagliacozzo I	27	E3
Táglio di Po I	21	E2
Tai di Cadore I	14	C2
Tailfingen D	4	C4
Taizé F	2	A1
Takácsi H	17	F4
Talloires F	10	C3
Tamsweg A	15	E4
Taninges F	11	D3
Tannheim A	5	E2
Taormina I	38	C3
Tapolca H	17	F3
Tapolcafő H	17	F4
Táranto I	32	C3
Tarasp CH	13	E4
Tarcento I	15	D2
Tarquinia I	26	C3
Tarsia I	32	B1
Tarvisio I	15	E2
Täsch CH	11	F3
Taufers/Tubre I	13	E4
Taufkirchen A	7	E3
Taufkirchen D	6	C3
Tauplitz A	7	F1
Taurianova I	34	C2
Tavannes CH	3	E2
Tavarnelle Val di Pesa I	23	F3
Tavaux F	2	B2
Taverna I	35	E3
Tavernelle I	24	B1
Taxenbach A	15	D4
Teano I	28	A1
Techendorf A	15	D3
Tegernsee D	6	B2
Teisendorf D	7	D2
Telč CZ	8	C4
Telese Terme I	28	B1
Telfs A	5	F2
Telti I	22	c4
Témpio Pausánia I	22	b4
Tende F	18	B2
Téramo I	28	A4
Terezino Polje HR	17	F1
Términi Imerese I	37	D4
Terminillo I	27	E4
Termoli I	28	C3
Terni I	27	D4
Ternitz A	9	D1
Terracina I	27	E1
Terralba I	22	a2
Terranova Pollino I	32	B2
Tertenía I	22	c2
Terz A	8	C2
Tét H	9	F1
Tettnang D	5	D3
Teufen CH	4	C2
Teulada I	22	a1
Thalwil CH	4	B2
Thann F	3	E3
Thannhausen D	5	E4
Théoule F	18	A1
Thiene I	21	D4
Thiersee A	6	C1
Thiesi I	22	b3
Thoissey F	10	A4
Thonon F	11	D4
Thun CH	3	F1
Thusis CH	12	C4
Tiana I	22	b2
Tiefencastel CH	13	D4
Tiengen D	4	B3
Tignes I	11	D2
Til-Châtel F	2	B3
Tione di Trento I	13	E2
Tirano I	13	D3
Tiriolo I	35	D3
Tirrénia I	23	D3
Titisee D	4	B3
Titovo Velenje SLO	16	B2
Tittling D	7	E4
Tittmoning D	7	D2
Tivoli I	27	D3
Toblach/Dobbiaco I	14	C3
Todi I	24	C1
Todtmoos D	4	A3
Todtnau D	4	A3
Tolentino I	25	D2
Tolfa I	26	C3
Tolmezzo I	15	D2
Tolmin SLO	15	E2
Tolve I	32	A3
Tonara I	22	b2
Tor Vaiánica I	27	D2
Torbole I	13	F2
Torino I	18	B4
Torino di Sangro Marina I	28	B3
Torony H	17	D4
Torre Annunziata I	31	D3
Torre Beretti I	19	D4
Torre Canne I	33	D3
Torre de' Passeri I	28	A3
Torre del Greco I	30	C3
Torre Faro I	34	C1
Torre Orsaia I	31	E2
Torre Pellice I	18	B3
Torremaggiore I	29	D2
Torri del Benaco I	13	E1
Torríglia I	19	E2
Torrita di Siena I	24	B2
Tortoli I	22	c2
Tortona I	19	E3
Tortorici I	38	B4
Toscolano Maderno I	13	E1
Tournus F	2	A1
Trabía I	37	D4
Trafoi I	13	E3
Traisen A	8	C2
Traiskirchen A	9	D2
Traismauer A	8	C3
Trakošćan HR	17	D2
Tramariglio I	22	a3
Tramelan CH	3	E2
Trani I	29	F1
Trápani I	36	B4
Traun A	7	F3
Traunkirchen A	7	E2
Traunreut D	6	C2
Traunstein D	6	C2

Travers CH 3 D2
Trebisacce I .... 32 BI
Trebnje SLO .... 16 BI
Třeboň CZ 8 B4
Trecastagni I 38 B3
Tremestieri I .... 34 BI
Tremezzo I 12 C2
Trento I 13 F2
Tresenda I 13 D3
Treuchtlingen D 6 A4
Trevi I .... 24 CI
Treviglio I .... 12 CI
Trevignano Romano I 26 C3
Treviso I 21 E4
Trévoux F 10 A3
Trhové Sviny CZ 8 A4
Triberg D 4 B4
Tricárico I 32 A3
Tricesimo I 15 D2
Trichiana I 14 B2
Trieben A .... 8 AI
Trieste I .... 15 EI
Trinita d'Agultu I 22 b4
Trinitapoli I .... 29 EI
Trino I 19 D4
Triponzo I .... 25 DI
Trnava SK 9 F3
Trocnov CZ 8 A4
Trofaiach A .... 8 BI
Troia I .... 29 DI
Troina I 38 B3
Trojane SLO 16 B2
Tropea I 34 C2
Trostberg D 6 C2
Trstín SK 9 F3
Tržič SLO 15 F2
Tübingen D 4 C4
Tubre/Taufers I 13 E4
Tullins F 10 B2
Tulln A 9 D3
Turckheim F 3 E4
Turi I 32 C4
Türkheim D 5 F3
Türnitz A 8 C2
Turrach A 15 E3
Tuscánia I 26 C4
Tuttlingen D 4 C3
Tutzing D 6 A2
Twimberg A 16 B3

Überlingen D 4 C3
Ucria I 38 B4
Udine I .... 15 DI
Ugento I 33 E2
Ugine F 10 C2
Uherské Hradiště CZ 9 F4
Uherský Brod CZ 9 F4
Ulm D 5 E4
Umbertide I 24 C2
Umhausen A .... 5 FI
Unter Pfaffenhofen D 6 A3
Unter-Schleissheim D 6 B3
Unterach A 7 E2
Unteruhldingen D 4 C3
Unterwasser CH 4 C2
Unterweissenbach A 8 B3
Unterwössen D 6 C2
Úras I 22 b2
Urbánia I 24 C3
Urbino I 24 C3
Uriage-les-Bains F .... 10 BI
Urnäsch CH 4 C2
Uster CH 4 B2
Uttendorf A 14 C4
Uttendorf A 7 D2
Utting D 6 A2

V

Vado Ligure I 19 D2
Vaduz FL 5 D2
Val d'Isère F 11 D2
Val Thorens F .... 10 CI
Val-Claret F 11 D2
Val-Suzon F 2 A3
Valbella CH 13 D4
Valberg F 18 A2
Valbonnais F .... 10 BI
Valdagno I 21 D4
Valdahon F 3 D2
Valdobbiádene I .... 14 BI
Váleggio S Mincio I 20 C3
Valentano I 26 C4
Valenza I 19 D4
Valfábbrica I 24 C2
Valguarnera Caropepe I 37 F3
Vallata I 31 E4
Vallecorsa I 27 E2
Vallelunga Pratameno I 37 E3
Valletta M .... 39 bI
Vallo di Lucania I 31 E2
Valloire F .... 10 CI
Vallorbe CH .... 3 DI
Vallorcine F 11 D3
Valmontone I 27 E2
Valmorel F 10 C2
Vals CH 12 C4
Valtournenche I 11 E2
Vámosszabadi H .... 9 FI
Varallo I 12 A2
Varaždin HR 17 D2
Varazze I 19 D2
Varces F .... 10 BI
Varenna I 12 C2
Varese I 12 B2
Varese Ligure I 19 F2
Várpslőd H 17 F4
Vars F 18 A3
Varzi I 19 E3
Vasto I 28 C3
Vasvár H 17 E3
Vát H 17 E4
Vauvillers F 2 C4
Vejano I 26 C3
Vel Lašče SLO .... 16 AI
Vel'ké Leváre SK 9 E3
Vela Luka HR 29 F4
Velden A 15 F3
Velden D 6 C3
Velešín CZ 8 A4
Velika Gorica HR .... 17 DI
Veliki Zdenci HR .... 17 EI
Velká nad Veličkou CZ 9 F4
Velké Němčice I 9 E4
Velletri I 27 D2
Venafro I .... 28 AI
Vence F .... 18 AI
Venézia I 21 E3
Venosa I 31 F4
Ventimíglia I .... 18 BI
Venzone I 15 D2
Verbania-Pallanza I 12 B2
Verbier I 11 E3
Vercelli I .... 12 AI
Vergato I .... 20 CI
Verona I 20 C4
Verrès I 11 E2
Verrières-de-Joux F 3 D2
Versoix CH 10 C3
Verucchio I 24 C3
Verzuolo I 18 B3
Vése H 17 F2
Veselí nad Moravou CZ 9 F4
Vesoul F 2 C3
Vestone I 13 B2
Vetralla I 26 C3
Vevey CH 11 D4

Veyrier F 10 C3
Vezzano I 13 F2
Viadana I 20 B2
Viaréggio I 23 D3
Vibo Valentia I 35 D2
Vič SLO 16 B3
Vicenza I 21 D4
Vico del Gargano I 29 E2
Vico Equense I 31 D3
Vicovaro I 27 E3
Victoria M 39 a2
Viechtach D 7 D4
Vienne F 10 A2
Vieste I 29 E2
Vietri di Potenza I 31 E3
Vietri sul Mare I 31 D3
Vif F .... 10 BI
Vigévano I .... 12 BI
Vignanello I 27 D3
Vignola I .... 20 CI
Villa Literno I 30 C4
Villa Minozzo I .... 20 BI
Villa Potenza I 25 E2
Villa San Giovanni I .... 34 CI
Villa Santa Maria I 28 B2
Villa Santina I 15 D2
Villa Vomano I 28 A4
Villach A 15 E3
Villacidro I 22 b2
Villafianca Tirrena I .... 34 BI
Villafranca di Verona I 20 C3
Villafrati I 37 D4
Villaggio Mancuso I 35 E3
Villamar I 22 b2
Villamassargia I .... 22 aI
Villanova Monteleone I 22 a3
Villapiana Scalo I .... 32 BI
Villaputzu I .... 22 cI
Villard-de-Lans F .... 10 BI
Villars CH 11 E3
Villars F 18 A2
Villars-les-Dombes F 10 A3
Villasalto I 22 b2
Villasimíus I .... 22 cI
Villasor I .... 22 bI
Villé F 3 F4
Villefranche I .... 18 AI
Villeneuve-Loubet F .... 18 AI
Villers-le-Lac F 3 D2
Villersexel F 3 D3
Villingen D 4 B4
Vilsbiburg D 6 C3
Vilshofen D 7 D3
Vimperk CZ 7 E4
Vinádio I 18 A2
Vinay F .... 10 AI
Vinchiaturo I .... 28 BI
Vinci I 23 F3
Vipiteno/Sterzing I 14 A3
Virgen A 14 C3
Virieu I 10 B2
Virieu-le-Grand F 10 B3
Virovitica HR .... 17 FI
Visp CH 11 F3
Visso I .... 25 DI
Viterbo I 26 C4
Vitis A 8 B4
Vitteaux F 2 A3
Vittel F 2 C4
Vittória I 38 A2
Vittório Véneto I .... 14 CI
Vittoriosa M .... 39 bI
Vizille F .... 10 BI
Vizzini I 38 B2
Vlachovo Březí CZ 7 E4
Vöcklabruck A 7 D2
Vodňany CZ 7 F4
Voghera I 19 E3
Vohburg D 6 B4
Vöhringen D 5 E4
Voiron F 10 B2
Voitsberg A 16 B3
Vojnik SLO 16 B2

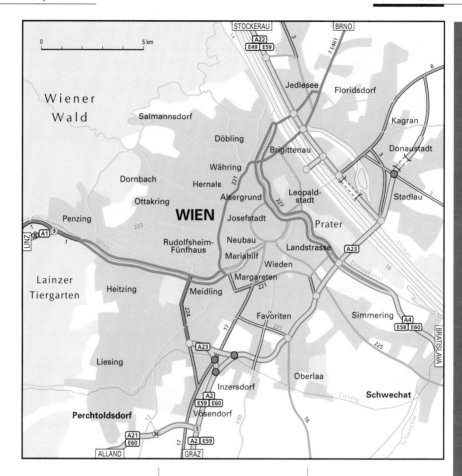

Volary *CZ*	7	F4
Volders *A*	14	B4
Völkermarkt *A*	16	A3
Volterra *I*	23	E2
Voltri *I*	19	D2
Volturara Appula *I*	28	C1
Vorau *A*	16	C4
Vorchdorf *A*	7	F2
Vordernberg *A*	8	B1
Vorderriss *D*	6	A1
Voreppe *F*	10	B2
Vransko *SLO*	16	B2
Vratno *HR*	17	D2
Vrbové *SK*	9	F3
Vrbovec *HR*	17	D1
Vrhnika *SLO*	15	F1
Vyšší Brod *CZ*	8	A3

W

Wädenswil *CH*	4	B2
Waging *D*	7	D2
Wagrain *A*	15	D4
Wahlwies *D*	4	C3
Waidhofen an der Thaya *A*	8	C4
Waidhofen an der Ybbs *A*	8	B2
Waidring *A*	6	C1

Walchensee *D*	6	A1
Walchsee *A*	6	C1
Wald *CH*	4	C2
Waldkirch *D*	4	A4
Waldkirchen *D*	7	E4
Waldkraiburg *D*	6	C3
Waldshut *D*	4	B3
Walenstadt *CH*	4	C2
Wallersdorf *D*	7	D4
Wangen *D*	5	D3
Wängi *CH*	4	C2
Warth *A*	5	E2
Wassen *CH*	12	B4
Wasserburg *D*	6	C2
Wattens *A*	14	B4
Wattwil *CH*	4	C2
Weesen *CH*	4	C2
Weggis *CH*	4	B1
Wegscheid *D*	7	E3
Wehr *D*	4	A3
Weichshofen *D*	6	C4
Weigetschlag *A*	8	A3
Weilheim *D*	6	A2
Weinfelden *CH*	4	C2
Weingarten *D*	5	D3
Weissbriach *A*	15	D3
Weissenbach *A*	5	E2
Weissenburg *D*	6	A4
Weissenhorn *D*	5	E4
Weissenkirchen *A*	8	C3

Weisskirchen *A*	16	B4
Weitra *A*	8	B3
Weiz *A*	16	C4
Welden *D*	5	F4
Wels *A*	7	F2
Welsberg/Monguelfo *I*	14	B3
Welschofen/Nova Levante *I*	14	A2
Weltenburg *D*	6	B4
Wemding *D*	6	A4
Wengen *CH*	11	F4
Wenns *A*	5	F1
Weppersdorf *A*	9	D1
Werfen *A*	7	D1
Wertach *D*	5	E2
Wertingen *D*	5	F4
Wessobrunn *D*	6	A2
Westendorf *A*	6	C1
Wetzikon *CH*	4	B2
Weyer-Markt *A*	8	A2
Weyregg *A*	7	E2
Wien *A*	9	D2
Wiener Neustadt *A*	9	D2
Wies *D*	5	F3
Wieselburg *A*	8	B2
Wiesmath *A*	9	D1
Wil *CH*	4	C2
Wildalpen *A*	8	B1
Wildhaus *CH*	4	C2
Wildon *A*	16	C3
Wilfersdorf *A*	9	E3

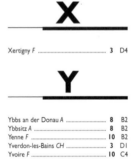

Wilhelmsburg A 8 C2
Wilhering A 7 F3
Willisau CH 4 A2
Windischgarsten A 8 A1
Winklern A 15 D3
Winterthur CH 4 B2
Wohlen CH 4 B2
Wolfach D 4 B4
Wolfegg D 5 D3
Wolfratshausen D 6 B2
Wolfsberg A 16 B3
Wolhusen CH 4 A2
Wolkenstein in Gardena/
   Selva di Val Gardena I 14 B3
Wolkersdorf A 9 D3
Wöllersdorf A 9 D2
Wolnzach D 6 B4
Worb CH 3 F1
Wörgl A 6 C1
Wörth D 6 C4
Wullowitz A 8 A3

X

Xertigny F 3 D4

Y

Ybbs an der Donau A 8 B2
Ybbsitz A 8 B2
Yenne F 10 B2
Yverdon-les-Bains CH 3 D1
Yvoire F 10 C4

Z

Žabno HR 17 E1
Zabok HR 16 C1
Zaga SLO 15 E2
Zagorje SLO 16 B2
Zagreb HR 17 D1
Zalaapáti H 17 E3
Zalabaksa H 17 D3
Zalabér H 17 E3
Zalaegerszeg H 17 E3
Zalakomár H 17 F2
Zalalövő H 17 E3
Zalaszentbalázs H 17 E2
Zapponeta I 29 E1
Zaprešić HR 16 C1
Željetava CZ 8 C4
Železná Ruda CZ 7 E4
Želin SLO 15 E2
Zelina HR 17 D1
Zell A 7 E3
Zell D 4 A3
Zell am See A 15 D4
Zell am Ziller A 14 B4
Želnava CZ 7 F4
Zeltweg A 16 B4
Zermatt CH 11 F3
Zernez CH 13 D4
Zidani Most SLO 16 B2
Židlochovice CZ 9 E4
Ziersdorf A 9 D3
Zinal CH 11 E3
Žiri SLO 15 F1
Zirl A 14 A4
Zistersdorf A 9 E3
Zizers CH 5 D1
Zlatá Koruna CZ 8 A4
Zlatar Bistrica HR 17 D1
Znojmo CZ 9 D4
Zofingen CH 4 A2
Zorneding D 6 B2
Zug CH 4 B2
Zuoz CH 13 D4
Zürich CH 4 B2
Zurrieq M 39 b1
Zürs A 5 E2
Zurzach CH 4 B3
Zusmarshausen D 5 F4
Žužemberk SLO 16 B1
Zweisimmen CH 11 E4
Zwettl A 8 B3
Zwettl an der Rodl A 8 A3
Zwiefalten D 5 D4
Zwiesel D 7 E4